LIZ E

QUICK GUIDES
Food Facts

LIZ EARLE'S
QUICK GUIDES
Food Facts

BOXTREE

First published in Great Britain in 1994 by Boxtree Limited,
Broadwall House, 21 Broadwall, London SE1 9PL

10 9 8 7 6 5 4 3 2 1

ISBN: 1 85283 543 5

Text design by Blackjacks
Cover design by Hammond Hammond

Printed and Bound in Great Britain by Cox & Wyman Ltd.,
Reading, Berkshire

A CIP catalogue entry for this book is available from
the British Library

For Lily, Guy, Lucy, Max, Oliver, Charlie, India, Alastair, Davina, Shannon, Maudie, Francesca, Mark, Davide and the health of our next generation.

Contents

ACKNOWLEDGEMENTS

I am grateful for Sarah Mobsby and Sarah Hamilton-Fleming for helping to produce this book.

With thanks to McCance and Widdowson, *The Composition of Foods*, 5th edition, and the Royal Society of Chemistry for nutritional references. Also to The Ministry of Agriculture, Fisheries and Food and the United States Department of Agriculture. Branded food references have been supplied by the manufacturers and I am especially grateful to all those listed in the tables.

Most manufacturers have been extremely helpful in the compilation of this Quick Guide. Notably Heinz, Marks and Spencer, Asda and Tesco. Unfortunately, others were not so forthcoming. It is incredible that a confectionary giant the size of Cadbury should be unable – or unwilling – to give the sugar content of their chocolate and sweets. What do they have to hide? It is also unbelievable that Pizza Hut have 'no interest in the nutrient content of pizzas' and that Coca Cola could not reveal their caffeine content. Their obstructiveness has made some of the calculations for this book difficult. However, the unhelpfulness of a few has been offset by the openness of many and I am indebted to the majority of food manufacturers for their kind co-operation.

Nutritional references are correct at time of publication but subject to change. Food labelling regulations may also change in the future, which means that although the data in this guide is correct it may not exactly correspond to the data listed on food labels.

Introduction

Food Facts is a unique and indispensable guide to all the foods we eat. It has been devised as the ideal pocket companion for the health-conscious shopper. Many books contain calorie values, but this *Quick Guide* gives you much more, including nutritional information about branded foods, pre-prepared meals and even many take-away foods.

We are all increasingly aware of the need to make healthier food choices for ourselves and our families. But how can we tell which options are best? Which fruits give us the most vitamins? How do the supermarket brands compare? This Quick Guide provides the know-how that will enable you to get the most from your food. Whether you are looking for foods that are low in calories, saturates, sodium and sugar, or prefer foods that are high in fibre, monosaturates, vitamin C, beta-carotene, folic acid, iron and calcium – *Food Facts* has the answers at your fingertips.

The foods in this book have been carefully chosen to provide the fullest representation of common ingredients and dishes. Likewise, the nutrient values given have also been selected as being the most relevant and useful in each category. The foods are divided into sections for easy reference. Each group of foods has been analysed for different nutrients, although all groups give their calorie (Kcal) content. Some food groups may list different vitamins and minerals depending on their type. For example, fruit and vegetables are generally very low in fat and so their minimal fat content is not listed. However, they do contain large amounts of important nutrients such as beta-carotene, which is not found in other food groups such as meat or alcoholic drinks.

Unlike other standard calorie counters, each section of this Quick Guide contains the most useful information and has been carefully planned to bring you the fullest and most relevant facts available. For example, the vague term 'carbohydrates' is not used in this guide. This is because the term carbohydrate includes sugars, so it is not generally that useful to know the overall carbohydrate content of foods. It is far more relevant to know how much of the carbohydrate content is made up of sugars and how much dietary fibre the food contains. Many of us look for foods that are low in sugar and high in dietary fibre. Unlike other booklets, this *Quick Guide* gives you these answers.

I hope you will find my *Quick Guide* as invaluable as I do and that it will help in the general quest for more informed consumer choices.

Liz Earle

How to Use
this Quick Guide

The foods in this guide are conveniently divided into several sections and listed in the left-hand column of each page. This is followed by the name of the manufacturer, where appropriate. Each of the subsequent columns is headed with the energy value (kilocalorie content) or nutrient. Unless specified, these values are always expressed as content per 100 grams of edible food. This means cooked rice; nuts, seeds and shellfish without shells; fruit without pits or inedible peel (such as bananas, avocado or mango) and meat without bones. In the case of fruit juices and alcoholic drinks, their nutritional values are also expressed per 100 grams. It is assumed that all fried foods are cooked in vegetable oil.

This Quick Guide Includes
the Following Categories:

CALORIES

These are a measurement of energy and are commonly expressed as kilocalories (Kcals). Energy may also be represented in kilojoules (kJ) but to avoid confusion these have not been included in this guide.

FATS

Of all the foods we should be most aware of, fat is the number one concern for a lean and healthy body. Fat contains the highest number of calories, at 9 Kcals per gram, than any other type of food. This compares to protein (4 Kcals per gram) and carbohydrate (3.75 Kcals per gram). Any weight-loss regime must be low in fat in order to be effective. However, there are several types of fat and these have been uniquely identified in this *Quick Guide.*

Most vegetable sources of fat contain monosaturated and polyunsaturated fats. Although these are all high in calories, they do not clog the arteries and lead to health problems such as heart disease and cancer in the same way as saturated fat can. Of the three different types of fats, saturated fat is the one we should avoid the most. Saturated fat is found in animal products. It is listed separately in these sections.

CHOLESTEROL

This is naturally present in animal products such as meat, egg yolks and cream. High-fat plant products such as vegetable oils and avocados do not contain cholesterol. Those with a history of heart disease are frequently advised to cut down on their cholesterol intake. A healthy diet should include less than 300 mg of cholesterol a day.

FIBRE

Many natural foods such as fruit, vegetables and whole grains are high in valuable fibre. A healthy diet should contain at least 15-20 grams of fibre a day. Eating more fibre and less fat is the most successful way to long-term weight-loss and better health.

There are two types of fibre. The first is soluble, which is soft and dissolves in the digestive tract. The second in insoluble fibre, which is hard and coarse (such as the outer skins of peas, beans and brown rice). This insoluble fibre provides bulk and helps to expel waste matter from the body. The figures given in this guide represent total fibre content, made up of both soluble and insoluble fibre. High fibre foods are frequently high in carbohydrates.

SUGARS

On food labels, sugars are usually listed under carbohydrates. This can be misleading, as we often want to increase our intake of energy-giving carbohydrates while decreasing the amount of high-calorie sugars. Many of us are concerned about the amount of sugar that is added to branded foods, which is why this *Quick Guide* lists sugars separately.

Sugars fall into two main groups: intrinsic and extrinsic. Intrinsic sugars are naturally present in foods such as fruits and vegetables. Extrinsic sugars are the refined sugars artificially added to foods and are less desirable. The figure given for Total Sugars represents both intrinsic and extrinsic sugars.

PROTEIN

Several food sections in this *Quick Guide* list protein when it is present in high quantities. However, there are two types of protein: complete and incomplete. Animal produce is a good source of complete protein. This means that it contains all the essential amino acids the body needs to obtain through food. Vegetable produce, such as grains, pulses and nuts are a good source of incomplete protein. This means that although they are listed as being high in protein, they lack several essential amino acids. For vegetarians to obtain a complete source of protein they need to combine two or more different sources of incomplete vegetable protein. This will ensure they receive their full quota of essential amino acids. For example, beans on toast, rice with pulses, lentils with grains or wholewheat pasta with nuts. For more information on vegetarian nutrition, see *Liz Earle's Quick Guide to Vegetarian Cookery.*

CALCIUM

This mineral is required from infancy to build strong teeth and bones. Calcium is also especially important for women during pregnancy, breastfeeding and the menopause. High calcium levels are believed to help prevent osteoporosis (brittle bones) in later life. The key to obtaining sufficient calcium lies in its absorption. Calcium needs vitamin D to be effectively absorbed. Its absorption many be blocked or slowed by the phytates naturally present in wheat bran. Phosphates that are added to fizzy drinks such as lemonade and cola also interfere with the absorption of calcium.

IRON

Low iron levels are a common cause of anaemia. This is especially prevalent in women with heavy periods due to their monthly blood loss. Iron is the most important part of haemoglobin, the red blood pigment that carries fresh oxygen supplies to every cell in the body. Healthy iron supplies are needed to maintain good health. The most absorbable form of iron is found in meat, so vegetarians must take care to eat plenty of other iron-rich foods to avoid a deficiency. Iron absorption is reduced by caffeine but increased by vitamin C. Therefore, drinking orange juice instead of coffee after a meal will boost your iron levels.

POTASSIUM

This mineral must be balanced with sodium (salt) in the body. An imbalance of sodium with low levels of potassium may lead to water retention, bloating, headaches and depression.

ZINC

Levels of this important mineral in the British diet frequently fall short of the World Health Organisation's targets. As animal produce is richest in zinc, vegetarians may risk a deficiency. Zinc is depleted by alcohol, aspirin and the contraceptive pill. Bran, coffee and dairy products can also interfere with zinc absorption. Modern farming methods depletes the zinc in soil so organically-grown produce is likely to contain higher levels.

SELENIUM

This mineral is toxic in high quantities, but tiny amounts are vitally important for good health. Selenium works in conjunction with vitamin E as an antioxidant nutrient, capable of neutralising a damaging excess of free radicals as they occur in the body. Selenium levels in the soil are reduced by fertilisers and removed from food by commercial processing.

VITAMIN A

This vitamin is essential for good eyesight and healthy skin. The principle source of vitamin A is called retinol and comes from animal sources, such as eggs and butter. However, vitamin A may also be made by the body from beta-carotene, an antioxidant nutrient found in colourful fruits and vegetables. Vitamin A is relatively stable in foods during cooking.

VITAMIN C

This commonly known vitamin has many functions in the body. It helps to maintain healthy skin tissues by making the protein called collagen. Vitamin C is a vital element for a healthy immune system and also functions as a powerful antioxidant. Although vitamin C is found in many fruits and vegetables, it is reduced by cooking, environmental pollution, smoking and drinking alcohol.

VITAMIN E

This is one of our most important vitamins. Recent research has revealed that vitamin E is a highly powerful antioxidant and plays an important role in protecting us against heart disease, cataracts and cancer. Vitamin E levels are reduced by food refining and exposure to heat and light.

BETA-CAROTENE

This nutrient is a plant pigment and is found in all brightly-coloured fruits and vegetables. As a general rule, the brighter the colour, the more beta-carotene it will contain. Beta-carotene is converted by the body into vitamin A. Any leftover is used as an important antioxidant and recent research shows that this may play a vitally important part in preventing cancer and heart disease. Beta-carotene is relatively stable during cooking and food processing.

FOLIC ACID

This nutrient is a member of the vitamin B complex family and part of a group of folic acid-related compounds known as folates. Folic acid is vitally important for women who become pregnant as it has been shown to help prevent neural tube defects (spina bifida) in babies. It is most useful during the first few weeks of pregnancy, before the foetal neural tubes close. For this reason, any women contemplating pregnancy or who might become pregnant should take folic acid supplements or ensure that her diet is rich in folates. This is very important and is the reason why folic acid has been included as a separate category in this *Quick Guide*. Folic acid is reduced by food processing, cooking at high temperatures and exposure to light.

ALCOHOL

Alcohol is not a nutrient. It reduces the level of vitamins in the body and causes dehydration.

CAFFEINE

Caffeine is not a nutrient and acts as a stimulant. It interferes with the absorption of vitamins and places a strain on the nervous system. Caffeine is also addictive.

Abbreviations Used in the Tables

mcg   *microgram*
mg   *milligram*
g   *gram*
ml   *millilitre*
nd   *nutrient may be present but no data is available*

Weights and Measures

IMPERIAL TO METRIC

1 ounce (oz)	=	*28.85 grams (g)*
1 pound (lb)	=	*453.60 grams (g)*
1 fluid ounce (fl oz)	=	*29.57 millilitres (ml)*
1 pint (pt)	=	*0.568 litre (l)*

METRIC TO IMPERIAL

100 grams (g)	=	*3.38 ounces (oz)*
1 kilogram (kg)	=	*2.2 pounds (lb)*
100 millilitres (ml)	=	*3.38 fluid ounces (fl oz)*
1 litre (l)	=	*1.76 pints (pt)*

Fruit

(edible part, raw unless stated)	Calories Kcals	Fibre g	Calcium mg	Iron mg	Potassium mg	Beta-carotene mcg	Vitamin C mg	Folic Acid mcg
FRUIT								
Apples, eating, average	47	1.8	4	0.1	120	19	6	1
eating, stewed	56	2	5	0.2	94	12	3	Trace
cooking, stewed	33	1.5	4	0.1	150	15	11	Trace
cooking, stewed with sugar	74	1.2	4	0.1	140	14	10	Trace
dried	243	nd	14	1.4	450	0	4	0
sauce, sweetened	76	1.2	4	0.4	61	6	2	1
sauce, unsweetened	43	1.5	3	0.1	75	18	10	1
Apricots	31	1.7	15	0.5	270	405	6	5
canned in juice	34	0.9	21	0.4	170	210	14	2
canned in syrup	63	0.9	19	0.2	150	155	1	11
dried	238	7.8	45	4.7	1377	nd	2	10
Avocado	190	3.4	11	0.4	450	11	4	8
Bananas	95	1.1	6	0.3	400	21	11	14
dried chips	518	6.6	17	1.2	535	164	6	14
Blackberries	25	3.1	41	0.7	160	80	15	34
stewed	21	2.4	35	0.6	140	68	10	5
Blackcurrants	28	3.6	60	1.3	370	100	200	nd
canned in juice	31	3.1	26	5.2	190	29	37	4
Blueberries	56	2.7	6	0.2	89	60	13	6

All amounts given per 100g, unless otherwise stated

(edible part, raw unless stated)	Calories	Fibre	Calcium	Iron	Potassium	Beta-carotene	Vitamin C	Folic Acid
	Kcals	g	mg	mg	mg	mcg	mg	mcg
Breadfruit	103	12.2	17	0.5	490	24	29	10
Cherries	48	0.9	13	0.2	210	25	11	5
canned in syrup	71	0.6	15	209	120	17	1	5
glacé	251	0.9	56	0.9	24	7	Trace	Trace
Clementines	37	1.1	31	0.1	130	75	54	33
Cranberries	49	4.2	7	0.2	71	30	14	2
sauce	151	1.2	4	0.2	26	nd	4	nd
Currants	267	1.9	93	1.3	720	6	Trace	4
Dates	253	7.4	41	0	657	nd	nd	Trace
dried	297	1.6	55	0.8	537	479	0	13
Dried mixed fruit	268	2.2	73	2.2	880	9	Trace	15
Exotic fruit salad (M&S)	52	1	nd	nd	nd	nd	nd	nd
Figs	74	6.4	36	0.4	232	84	2	6
dried	227	7.5	250	4.2	970	64	1	9
Fruit salad (M&S)	48	1.4	nd	nd	nd	nd	nd	nd
Gooseberries	19	2.4	28	0.3	210	110	14	8
stewed with sugar	54	1.9	19	0.3	140	41	11	6
canned in syrup	73	1.7	12	0.2	66	18	27	2
Grapefruit	30	1.3	23	0.1	200	17	36	0
canned in juice	30	0.4	22	0.3	72	Trace	33	6

All amounts given per 100g, unless otherwise stated

Fruit

Fruit

(edible part, raw unless stated)	Calories Kcals	Fibre g	Calcium mg	Iron mg	Potassium mg	Beta-carotene mcg	Vitamin C mg	Folic Acid mcg
Grapefruit								
canned in syrup	60	0.6	17	0.7	79	Trace	30	4
Grapes, average	60	0.7	13	0.3	210	17	3	2
Guava	26	3.7	13	0.4	230	435	230	nd
Kiwi fruit	49	1.9	25	0.4	290	37	59	nd
Lemons	19	nd	85	0.5	150	18	58	nd
Limes	30	0.5	33	0.6	102	6	29	8
Lychees	58	0.7	6	0.5	160	0	45	nd
canned in syrup	68	0.5	4	0.7	75	0	8	nd
Mandarins, canned in juice	32	0.3	17	0.5	85	95	20	12
canned in syrup	52	0.2	17	0.2	49	105	15	12
Mangoes	57	2.6	12	0.7	180	1800	37	nd
pickle	76	2.5	4	1.9	29	48	1	9
Melons, Canteloupe-type	19	1	20	0.3	210	1000	26	5
Galia	24	0.4	13	0.2	150	nd	15	3
Honeydew	28	0.6	9	0.1	210	48	9	2
Watermelon	31	0.1	7	0.3	100	230	8	2
Mixed peel	231	nd	130	1.3	21	Trace	Trace	nd
Mixed dried fruit	237	5.7	nd	nd	nd	nd	nd	nd
Nectarines	40	2.2	7	0.4	170	58	37	Trace

All amounts given per 100g, unless otherwise stated

(edible part, raw unless stated)	Calories Kcals	Fibre g	Calcium mg	Iron mg	Potassium mg	Beta-carotene mcg	Vitamin C mg	Folic Acid mcg
Olives, green in brine	103	2.9	61	1	91	180	0	Trace
Oranges	37	1.7	47	0.1	150	28	54	31
Papaya (or paw-paw)	36	2.2	23	0.5	200	810	60	1
Passion fruit	36	3.3	11	1.3	200	750	23	nd
Peaches	33	1.5	7	0.4	160	58	31	3
canned in juice	39	0.8	4	0.4	170	67	6	2
canned in syrup	55	0.9	3	0.2	110	75	5	7
Pears, average	40	2.2	11	0.2	150	18	6	2
canned in juice	33	1.4	6	0.2	81	Trace	3	4
canned in syrup	50	1.1	6	0.2	68	Trace	2	3
Pineapple	41	1.2	18	0.2	160	18	12	5
canned in juice	47	0.5	8	0.5	71	12	11	1
canned in syrup	64	0.7	6	0.2	79	11	13	1
Plantains, cooked	116	2.3	2	0.6	465	544	11	26
Plums, average	36	2.3	13	0.4	240	295	4	3
Pomegranate	68	0.7	3	0.3	259	0	6	6
Prunes	141	5.7	34	2.6	760	140	Trace	3
canned in juice	80	4.6	nd	nd	nd	nd	nd	nd
canned in syrup	97	4.6	nd	nd	nd	nd	nd	nd
Quince	57	1.9	11	0.7	197	24	15	3

All amounts given per 100g, unless otherwise stated

Fruit

Fruit

FOOD FACTS

(edible part, raw unless stated)	Calories Kcals	Fibre g	Calcium mg	Iron mg	Potassium mg	Beta-carotene mcg	Vitamin C mg	Folic Acid mcg
Raisins	272	2	46	3.8	1020	12	1	10
Raspberries	25	2.5	25	0.7	170	6	32	33
canned in syrup	88	1.5	14	1.7	100	3	7	10
Rhubarb	7	1.4	93	0.3	290	60	6	7
stewed	7	1.3	35	0.1	230	30	5	4
stewed with sugar	48	1.2	33	0.1	210	28	5	4
Satsumas	36	1.3	31	0.1	130	75	27	33
Star fruit	24	1.8	5	0.3	99	1790	26	9
Strawberries	27	1.1	16	0.4	160	8	77	20
canned in syrup	65	0.7	11	1.1	87	4	29	6
Sultanas	275	2	64	2.2	1060	12	Trace	27
Tangerines	35	1.3	42	0.3	160	97	30	21

All amounts given per 100g, unless otherwise stated

VEGETABLES

(boiled in water unless stated)	Calories	Fibre	Calcium	Iron	Potassium	Beta-carotene	Vitamin C	Folic Acid
	Kcals	g	mg	mg	mg	mcg	mg	mcg
Acorn squash	56	2.1	44	0.9	437	nd	11	19
Alfalfa sprouts, raw	29	2.2	32	1	79	96	8	36
Artichoke (globe)	50	3.3	45	1.3	354	83	10	51
Asparagus	26	1.4	25	0.6	220	530	10	155
Aubergine, fried	302	2.3	8	0.5	170	125	1	5
Bamboo shoots	12	1.8	12	0.2	533	11	0	2.3
raw	27	2.6	13	0.5	533	11	4	7.1
Beansprouts, raw	30	1.5	13	0.9	149	12	13	61
boiled	21	2.2	12	0.7	101	12	11	29
Beetroot	46	1.9	29	0.8	510	27	5	110
pickled, drained	28	1.7	19	0.5	190	Trace	nd	2
Broad beans, frozen, boiled	81	6.5	56	1.6	280	225	8	32
Broccoli	24	2.3	40	1	170	475	44	64
raw	33	2.6	56	1.7	370	575	87	90
Brussel sprouts	35	3.1	20	0.5	310	320	60	110
raw	42	4.1	26	0.02	450	215	115	135
Butternut squash, baked	40	1.7	41	0.6	284	nd	15	12
Cabbage (average)	16	2.4	33	0.3	120	210	20	29

All amounts given per 100g, unless otherwise stated

Vegetables

Vegetables

(boiled in water unless stated)	Calories Kcals	Fibre g	Calcium mg	Iron mg	Potassium mg	Beta-carotene mcg	Vitamin C mg	Folic Acid mcg
Cabbage,								
(average), raw	26	1.8	52	0.02	270	385	49	75
red, raw	27	2	51	0.5	206	4	57	21
Savoy, raw	27	2.1	36	0.4	230	78	31	80
white, raw	27	2.1	49	0.5	240	40	35	34
Carrots	24	2.5	24	0.4	120	7560	2	16
raw	35	2.4	25	0.3	170	8115	6	12
canned, drained	20	1.9	25	0.6	110	3370	1	6
Cauliflower	28	1.6	17	0.4	120	60	27	51
raw	34	1.8	21	0.7	120	50	43	51
Celery	8	1.2	45	0.3	230	50	4	10
raw	7	1.1	41	0.4	320	50	8	16
Chicory, raw	11	0.9	21	0.4	170	120	5	14
Courgettes	19	1.2	19	0.6	210	440	11	31
raw	18	0.9	25	0.8	360	610	21	52
fried	63	1.2	38	1.4	490	500	15	42
Cucumber, raw	10	0.6	18	0.3	140	60	2	9
pickled (M&S)	40	0.5	nd	nd	nd	nd	nd	nd
Fennel	11	2.3	20	0.2	300	60	2	26
Garlic	98	4.1	19	1.9	620	Trace	17	5

All amounts given per 100g, unless otherwise stated

(boiled in water unless stated)	Calories Kcals	Fibre g	Calcium mg	Iron mg	Potassium mg	Beta-carotene mcg	Vitamin C mg	Folic Acid mcg
Gherkins, pickled, drained	14	1.2	20	0.7	110	2	1	6
Kale	24	2.8	150	2	160	3375	71	86
raw	33	3.1	130	1.7	450	3145	110	120
Leeks	21	1.7	20	0.7	150	575	7	40
Lettuce (average), raw	14	0.9	28	0.7	220	355	5	55
iceberg, raw	13	0.6	19	0.4	160	50	3	53
Mange-tout	26	2.2	35	0.8	170	665	28	6
raw	32	2.3	44	0.8	200	695	54	10
stir-fried	71	2.4	46	0.8	210	725	51	9
Marrow	9	1	14	0.1	110	110	3	15
Mushrooms	11	1.1	5	0.5	250	0	1	8
raw	13	1.1	6	0.6	320	Trace	1	44
fried	157	1.5	8	1	340		1	11
fried in butter	157	1.5	11	1	340	85	1	11
Mustard and cress, raw	13	1.1	50	1	110	1280	33	60
Okra	28	3.6	120	0.6	310	465	16	46
raw	31	4	160	1.1	330	515	21	88
stir-fried	269	6.3	220	1.5	480	560	21	83
Onions	17	0.7	19	0.3	90	5	3	9
raw	36	1.4	25	0.3	160	10	5	17

All amounts given per 100g, unless otherwise stated

27

Vegetables

Vegetables

FOOD FACTS

(boiled in water unless stated)	Calories Kcals	Fibre g	Calcium mg	Iron mg	Potassium mg	Beta-carotene mcg	Vitamin C mg	Folic Acid mcg
Onions								
fried	164	3.1	47	0.8	370	40	3	38
pickled, drained	24	1.2	22	0.2	93	10	Trace	14
Original mixed vegetables	50	3.1	nd	nd	nd	nd	nd	nd
Parsnips	66	4.7	50	0.6	350	30	10	48
Peas	79	4.5	19	1.5	230	250	16	27
frozen, boiled	69	5.1	35	1.6	150	405	12	47
petit-pois, frozen, boiled	49	4.5	42	1.6	130	405	8	50
canned, drained	80	5.1	30	1.9	130	450	1	20
mushy, canned	81	1.8	14	1.3	170	nd	Trace	nd
mushy, low salt (Asda)	82	7.9	nd	nd	nd	nd	nd	nd
yellow, split	324	5.9	nd	nd	nd	nd	nd	nd
Peppers, green	18	1.8	9	0.4	140	240	69	19
green, raw	15	1.6	8	0.4	120	265	120	36
red	34	1.7	9	0.3	180	3780	81	11
red, raw	32	1.6	8	0.3	160	3840	140	11
Plantain	112	1.2	5	0.5	400	350	9	22
fried	267	2.3	6	0.8	610	nd	12	37
Potatoes, without skins	72	1.2	5	0.4	280	Trace	6	26
Alphabites (Walls)	154	1.8	nd	nd	nd	nd	nd	nd

All amounts given per 100g, unless otherwise stated

	Calories	Fibre	Calcium	Iron	Potassium	Beta-carotene	Vitamin C	Folic Acid
	Kcals	g	mg	mg	mg	mcg	mg	mcg
baked with skin	136	2.7	5	0.4	280	Trace	14	44
canned (M&S)	48	2.5	nd	nd	nd	nd	nd	nd
roast	149	1.8	8	0.7	570	Trace	8	36
oven (Walls)	165	1.9	nd	nd	nd	nd	nd	nd
mashed with milk and butter	104	1.1	13	0.4	260	21	5	24
new with skins	66	1.5	13	1.6	430	Trace	15	10
potato skins (M&S)	170	2.5	nd	nd	nd	nd	nd	nd
chips (homemade), fried	189	2.2	11	0.8	660	Trace	9	43
chips, crinkle cut (Asda)	173	3	nd	nd	nd	nd	nd	nd
chips, frozen, fried	273	2.4	15	0.9	710	Trace	16	30
just bake chips, frozen (M&S)	166	2.3	nd	nd	nd	nd	nd	nd
low fat bake chips, frozen (M&S)	133	1.7	nd	nd	nd	nd	nd	nd
oven chips, frozen, baked	162	2	12	0.8	530	Trace	12	21
instant mashed mix	318	0.9	nd	nd	nd	nd	6	nd
salad, with mayonnaise	133	0.7	nd	nd	nd	nd	nd	nd
salad, reduced calorie (Asda)	90	0.8	nd	nd	nd	nd	nd	nd
Pumpkin	13	1.1	23	0.1	84	955	7	10
Quorn (micro-protein), as bought	86	4.8	nd	nd	nd	0	0	7
Radish, raw	12	0.9	19	0.6	240	Trace	17	38
Runner beans, tinned	24	3.2	nd	nd	nd	nd	nd	nd

(boiled in water unless stated)

All amounts given per 100g, unless otherwise stated

Vegetables

Vegetables

FOOD FACTS

(boiled in water unless stated)	Calories	Fibre	Calcium	Iron	Potassium	Beta-carotene	Vitamin C	Folic Acid
	Kcals	g	mg	mg	mg	mcg	mg	mcg
Salad, four leaf mix (Asda)	76	1.5	nd	nd	nd	nd	nd	nd
herb salad (Asda)	17	1.1	nd	nd	nd	nd	nd	nd
swede & sultana (Asda)	337	59.7	nd	nd	nd	nd	nd	nd
Seaweed, agar, dried	306	3.2	626	21.4	1126	170	0	581
dulse, dried	298	5.7	372	25	244	171	5	337
Irishmoss, raw	49	3.5	72	8.9	63	814	11	182
kelp, dried	43	4.2	168	2.8	89	171	5	180
wakami, dried	45	4.2	150	2.2	50	814	3	195
Shallot, raw	72	nd	37	1.2	334	nd	8	34
Spinach	19	2.1	160	1.6	230	3840	8	90
frozen, boiled	21	2.1	150	1.7	340	3840	6	90
raw	25	2.1	170	2.1	500	3535	26	150
Spring greens	20	2.6	75	1.4	160	2270	77	66
raw	33	3.4	210	3	370	2630	180	92
Spring onions, raw	23	1.5	39	1.9	260	620	26	54
Swede	11	0.7	26	0.1	86	165	15	18
Sweet potato	84	2.3	23	0.7	300	3960	17	8
Sweetcorn, on-the-cob	66	1.3	2	0.3	140	71	4	20
kernels, frozen, boiled	81	2.2	2	0.3	139	nd	3	28
kernels, canned, drained	122	1.4	4	0.5	220	110	1	8

All amounts given per 100g, unless otherwise stated

Vegetables

(boiled in water unless stated)	Calories Kcals	Fibre g	Calcium mg	Iron mg	Potassium mg	Beta-carotene mcg	Vitamin C mg	Folic Acid mcg
Sweetcorn, baby, canned, drained	23	1.5	8	1.2	180	140	14	nd
Tomatoes, raw	17	1	7	0.5	250	640	17	17
fried	91	1.3	12	0.5	300	765	16	17
grilled	49	2.9	20	1.4	720	1840	44	44
canned	16	0.7	12	0.4	250	220	12	11
purée	68	2.8	48	1.6	1150	1300	38	54
Turnip	12	1.9	45	0.2	200	20	10	8
Turnip greens	20	3.1	137	0.8	203	0	27	119
Water chestnuts, raw	106	nd	11	0.1	584	nd	4	16
canned	50	2.2	4	0.9	118	0	1	5.8
Watercress, raw	22	1.5	170	2.2	230	2520	62	nd
Yam	133	1.4	12	0.4	260	Trace	4	6

All amounts given per 100g, unless otherwise stated

Pulses

(dried, soaked & boiled unless stated)	Calories	Total Fat	Fibre	Protein	Calcium	Iron	Zinc	Folic Acid
	Kcals	g	g	g	mg	mg	mg	mg
PULSES								
Aduki beans	127	0.1	6.2	7.5	27	2	1.8	121.3
Baked beans, canned in tomato sauce	79	0.5	7.3	5.1	nd	nd	nd	nd
reduced sugar and salt	61	0.5	7.3	5.1	nd	nd	nd	nd
Heinz	75	0.2	3.7	4.7	nd	1.4	0.5	nd
Black beans	132	0.5	4.2	8.8	27	2.1	1.1	148.8
Black-eye beans	116	0.7	3.5	8.8	21	1.9	1.1	210
canned, drained	77	0.5	4.6	5.9	15	1.5	0.6	12
Butter beans	286	1.1	14.4	19.1	nd	nd	nd	nd
Chick peas	121	2.1	4.3	8.4	46	2.1	1.2	54
canned, drained	115	2.9	4.1	7.2	43	1.5	0.8	11
Haricot beans	97	0.5	7.4	6.6	nd	nd	nd	nd
Hummus (chick peas)	187	12.6	2.4	7.6	41	1.9	1.4	30
Lentils, green	105	0.7	3.8	8.8	22	3.5	1.4	5
red	100	0.4	1.9	7.6	16	2.4	1	5
Miso (fermented soya beans)	206	20.2	1.2	17.2	372	4.8	2	26.8
Mung beans	91	0.4	0.1	7.6	24	1.4	0.9	35
Pinto beans	137	0.5	7.4	8.2	48	2.6	1.1	171.9
Red kidney beans	103	0.5	0.1	8.4	37	2.5	1	42

All amounts given per 100g, unless otherwise stated

(dried, soaked & boiled unless stated)	Calories Kcals	Total Fat g	Fibre g	Protein g	Calcium mg	Iron mg	Zinc mg	Folic Acid mg
canned, drained	100	0.6	0.1	6.9	71	2	0.7	8
Refried beans	107	1.1	4.6	6.2	46	1.8	1.4	83.4
Soya beans	141	7.3	0.9	14	83	3	0.9	54
Soybean cake	102	4.7	0	10.9	164	2.6	1	25.8
Soya flour	447	23.5	11.2	36.8	210	6.9	3.9	345
low fat	352	7.2	13.5	45.3	240	9.1	3.2	410
Soya milk	32	1.9	Trace	2.9	13	0.4	0.2	19
Soya dessert topping, 100ml (Sains)	178	17.6	0.1	3	nd	nd	nd	nd
Soya yoghurt	66	4.9	nd	5	nd	nd	nd	nd
Split green peas	115	0.5	5.3	8	11	1.7	1.1	64.5
Tempeh	199	7.7	nd	19	9.3	2.3	1.8	52
Tofu (soya bean), steamed	73	4.2	0.5	8.1	510	1.2	2	15
steamed and fried	261	17.7	nd	23.5	1480	3.5	2	27
Four bean salad (Asda)	136	1.23	nd	nd	nd	nd	nd	nd

All amounts given per 100g, unless otherwise stated

Pulses

Grains and Flours

	Calories	Total Fat	Fibre	Protein	Calcium	Iron	Zinc	Folic Acid
	Kcals	g	g	g	mg	mg	mg	mcg
GRAINS AND FLOURS								
Barley, pearl	336	1.3	3.4	9.2	23	2.6	0.8	3.7
flour	358	1.7	18	10.2	41	4.3	2.5	48
Bran, wheat	206	5.5	36.4	14.1	110	12.9	16.2	260
Bulgar wheat	359	1.7	9.1	9.7	nd	nd	nd	nd
Buckwheat groats, cooked	92	0.6	2	3.4	7	0.8	0.6	18.1
flour	335	3.1	14.1	12.6	41	4.1	3.1	53.3
Couscous	112	0.2	4.6	3.8	8	0.4	0.3	15
Custard powder	354	0.7	0.1	0.6	15	1.4	0.3	Trace
Maize kernels	365	4.7	11.1	9.4	7	2.7	2.2	19
popcorn, popped (plain)	387	5	8	12.7	11	2.7	4.1	18
cornflour	354	0.7	0.1	0.6	15	1.4	0.3	Trace
cornmeal	366	1.6	0.8	8.5	5	4.1	0.7	47.9
Millet, cooked	119	1	4.8	3.5	3	0.6	0.9	19
Oats, uncooked	389	6.9	13.3	16.9	54	4.7	4	55.8
oatmeal	375	9.2	7.1	11.2	52	3.8	3.3	60
rolled oats	371	3.8	0.7	10.1	39	3.5	nd	nd
Pasta, white, boiled	132	1.1	1.1	5.2	6	0.5	0.6	7
brown, boiled	124	0.5	5.6	2.3	10.8	1.3	0.8	5

All amounts given per 100g, unless otherwise stated

	Calories	Total Fat	Fibre	Protein	Calcium	Iron	Zinc	Folic Acid
	Kcals	g	g	g	mg	mg	mg	mcg
ribbons (M&S)	366	3	3.6	14	nd	nd	nd	nd
spinach, boiled	130	0.9	1.1	5.1	7	1.1	0.6	7
swirls (M&S)	366	3	3.6	14	nd	nd	nd	nd
twists, tri-colour	346	1.5	3	12	nd	nd	nd	nd
Quinoa	374	5.8	5.2	13	60	9.2	3.3	49
Rice, brown, boiled	141	1.1	0.8	2.6	4	0.5	0.7	10
white (Carolina), boiled	138	1.3	0.1	2.6	18	0.2	0.7	4
easy cook	336	1	0.5	7.3	nd	nd	nd	nd
Basmati	333	0.5	0.5	7.4	nd	nd	nd	nd
flour	371	1	0	6	36	10	nd	nd
flour, brown	363	2.8	3.4	7.2	11.4	2	2.4	15.8
long grain wild rice (M&S)	325	0.8	2.2	8.4	nd	md	nd	nd
cakes, brown, plain	389	3.3	2.2	7.8	11	1.4	3	22.2
Rye flour	354	1.8	12.7	9.4	24	2.1	2	19.6
Sago	355	0.2	11.7	0.2	10	1.2	nd	Trace
Semolina	360	1	nd	12.7	17	4.3	1	72
Tapioca	359	0.1	0.4	0.4	8	0.3	nd	Trace
Wheat	349	2.1	1.8	12.4	38	3.8	nd	nd
flour, brown	323	1.8	6.4	12.6	130	3.2	1.9	51
flour, white, plain	341	1.3	3.1	9.4	140	2	0.6	22

All amounts given per 100g, unless otherwise stated

Grains and Flours

Grains and Flours

	Calories	Total Fat	Fibre	Protein	Calcium	Iron	Zinc	Folic Acid
	Kcals	g	g	g	mg	mg	mg	mcg
Wheat								
flour, white, self-raising	330	1.2	3.1	8.9	350	2	0.6	19
flour, wholemeal	310	2.2	9	12.7	38	3.9	2.9	57
Wheatgerm	302	9.2	15.6	26.7	55	8.5	17	331
Wild rice	366	1.6	0.8	8.5	5	4.1	0.7	47.9

All amounts given per 100g, unless otherwise stated

BREAD

	Calories	Total Fat	Fibre	Total Sugars	Calcium	Iron	Zinc	Folic Acid
	Kcals	g	g	g	mg	mg	mg	mcg
Bagel	275	1.5	nd	nd	75	3.6	0.9	23
Baguette	245	0.3	2.4	1.4	nd	nd	nd	nd
Breadsticks	383	2.9	2	nd	28	0.9	nd	nd
Brioche loaf (M&S)	340	17.4	2.2	4.4	nd	nd	nd	nd
Brown bread, average	218	2	3.5	3	100	2.2	1.1	40
Heinz (Weight Watchers)	212	1.9	4.5	1.8	nd	2	1.5	30
Ciabatta, olive, (M&S)	255	5.4	2.1	2.3	nd	nd	nd	nd
toasted	272	2.1	4.5	4.5	140	2.7	1.3	44
Chapatis	328	12.8	nd	1.8	66	2.3	1.1	15
Cracked wheat bread	250	3.1	nd	nd	69	2.9	1.5	40
Croissants	360	20.3	1.6	1	80	2	0.9	73
Croutons	315	3.7	1.6	nd	140	3.3	0.9	47.9
Currant bread	289	7.6	nd	1.6	86	1.6	0.7	19
toasted	323	8.5	nd	14.4	96	1.8	0.8	21
French stick	270	2.7	1.5	1.9	130	2.1	0.7	24
French toast	281	17.9	3.2	nd	119	1.4	0.8	23
Garlic baguette (M&S)	377	24.2	1.6	3	nd	nd	nd	nd
Granary bread	235	2.7	4.3	2.2	77	2.7	1.5	90

All amounts given per 100g, unless otherwise stated

Bread and Cereals

Bread and Cereals

	Calories	Total Fat	Fibre	Total Sugars	Calcium	Iron	Zinc	Folic Acid
	Kcals	g	g	g	mg	mg	mg	mcg
Hovis	212	2	3.3	1.8	120	3.7	2.1	39
M&S	222	3.1	4.1	4.5	nd	nd	nd	nd
Malt bread	268	2.4	nd	26.1	110	2.8	1.1	30
Naan bread	336	12.5	1.9	5.5	160	1.3	0.8	14
M&S	235	2.1	3.7	5.1	nd	nd	nd	nd
Pitta bread	265	1.2	2.2	2.4	91	1.7	0.6	21
M&S	261	1.2	2	1.6	nd	nd	nd	nd
Asda	261	1.2	nd	2	nd	nd	nd	nd
wholemeal	232	1.8	nd	7.1	nd	nd	nd	nd
Poppadoms, fried	369	16.9	7.9	Trace	69	11	2.5	28
M&S	476	28.4	nd	1.3	nd	nd	nd	nd
Rye bread	219	1.7	4.4	1.8	80	2.5	1.3	24
White bread, average	235	1.9	1.5	2.6	110	1.65	0.6	29
toasted	265	1.6	1.8	3.7	120	1.7	0.6	21
fried	503	32.2	1.6	3.1	100	1.5	0.5	9
Heinz (Weight Watchers)	231	1.6	2.8	1.7	nd	1.5	0.8	21
Wholemeal, average	215	2.5	5.8	1.8	54	2.7	1.8	39

All amounts given per 100g, unless otherwise stated

CEREALS

	Calories	Total Fat	Fibre	Total Sugars	Calcium	Iron	Zinc	Folic Acid
	Kcals	g	g	g	mg	mg	mg	mcg
All-Bran (Kelloggs)	261	3.4	24.5	19	69	12	6.7	190
Bran Flakes (Kelloggs)	318	1.9	13	18.7	50	20	3.3	250
Asda	330	3.2	14.6	18.8	nd	20	nd	nd
unsweetened bran (M&S)	320	5.4	11.2	18.1	nd	nd	nd	nd
Bran cereal, high fibre (Asda)	306	4.2	19.8	19.8	nd	9	nd	nd
Cheerios	400	6.7	7.3	nd	163	13.3	2.6	60
Coco Pops	384	1	0.6	38.2	20	6.7	0.8	250
Common Sense Oat Bran Flakes	357	4	10	16.8	50	6.7	2.5	250
Corn Flakes (Kelloggs)	360	0.7	0.9	8.2	15	6.7	0.2	250
Crunchy Nut Corn Flakes (Kelloggs)	398	4	0.8	36.3	18	6.7	0.3	250
Crispy nut cornflakes (Asda)	391	1	0.9	nd	14	nd	nd	200
Frosties	377	0.5	0.6	41.9	11	6.7	0.1	250
Honey nut loops (Sains)	383	4.3	4.6	36.3	nd	nd	nd	nd
Lite crunchy cereal (M&S)	324	7.4	22.9	30.4	nd	nd	nd	nd
Malted wheat flakes	353	1.85	nd	nd	nd	nd	nd	nd
Malted wheaties (Asda)	352	1.8	8.1	14.1	nd	nd	nd	nd
Fruit 'n' Fibre	349	4.7	7	24.4	40	6.7	1.7	250

All amounts given per 100g, unless otherwise stated

Bread and Cereals

Bread and Cereals

	Calories	Total Fat	Fibre	Total Sugars	Calcium	Iron	Zinc	Folic Acid
	Kcals	g	g	g	mg	mg	mg	mcg
Muesli, Swiss style	363	5.9	6.4	26.2	110	5.8	2.3	140
with no added sugar	366	7.8	7.6	15.7	47	3.5	2.1	nd
luxury (Asda)	396	11.2	5.9	28.7	nd	nd	nd	nd
Oat and Wheat Bran	325	3.5	17.9	16.7	70	45	4	nd
Instant hot oats (Asda)	391	7.8	7.3	1.9	nd	nd	nd	nd
Crunchy oat cereal, honey & almond (Asda)	383	12	12	nd	nd	nd	nd	nd
Porridge, with water	49	1.1	0.8	Trace	7	0.5	0.4	4
with whole milk	116	5.1	0.8	4.7	120	0.6	0.8	7
Puffed Wheat	321	1.3	5.6	0.3	26	4.6	2.8	19
Raisin Splitz	337	2	8	18.2	50	5.1	1.8	190
Ready Brek	373	7.8	7.2	1.7	65	13.2	2.7	53
Rice Krispies (Kelloggs)	369	0.9	0.7	10.6	10	6.7	0.9	250
Rice snaps (Asda)	382	1.4	0.8	10.1	nd	14	nd	200
Ricicles	381	0.5	0.4	41.9	10	6.7	0.6	250
Shredded Wheat	325	3	9.8	0.8	38	4.2	2.3	29
Shreddies	331	1.5	9.5	10.2	40	2.8	2.5	28
Special K	377	1	2	17.2	70	13.3	1.9	330
Start	0.55	1.7	5.7	29.1	40	15	18.7	375
Sugar Puffs	324	0.8	3.2	56.5	14	2.1	1.5	12

All amounts given per 100g, unless otherwise stated

	Calories	Total Fat	Fibre	Total Sugar	Calcium	Iron	Zinc	Folic Acid
	Kcals	g	g	g	mg	mg	mg	mcg
Sultana Bran	303	1.6	10	28.6	51	15	2.8	250
Weetabix	352	2.7	9.7	5.2	35	7.4	2	50
Weetaflakes	359	2.8	8.8	20.3	29	11.5	1.7	42
Weetos	372	2.7	6.3	33.2	65	10.9	2.3	2

All amounts given per 100g, unless otherwise stated

Bread and Cereals

Milk and Dairy

MILK AND DAIRY

	Calories	Total Fat	Saturated Fat	Cholesterol	Protein	Total Sugars	Calcium	Sodium (Salt)
	Kcals	g	g	mg	g	g	mg	mg
Buttermilk	40	0.9	0.5	4	3.3	4.8	116	105
Cheese, Bavarian (M&S)	305	24	15.8	nd	14	0.1	nd	1300
Brie	319	26.9	16.8	100	19.3	Trace	540	700
Caerphilly (Tesco)	373	31.3	20.7	nd	22.8	0.1	nd	480
Cambozola	432	42	26.9	nd	13.5	0	nd	800
Camembert	297	23.7	14.8	75	20.9	Trace	350	650
Cheddar, average	412	34.4	21.7	100	25.5	0.1	720	670
Cheddar, vegetarian	425	35.7	22.5	105	25.8	Trace	690	670
Cheddar, reduced fat	261	15	9.4	43	31.5	Trace	840	670
Cheddar, reduced fat, (M&S)	327	23	14	nd	30	0.1	nd	700
Cheddar, reduced fat slices (M&S)	327	23	14	nd	30	0	nd	700
Cheddar spread (M&S)	280	21	14	nd	15	7	nd	600
Cheddar, smoked (M&S)	412	34.4	21.7	nd	25.5	0.1	nd	700
Cheshire	387	30.6	19.4	102	23.3	nd	641	697
chèvre	327	28.2	15	90	18.3	nd	103	582
cottage cheese, plain	98	3.9	2.4	13	13.8	2.1	73	380
cottage cheese, very low fat, (M&S)	81	0.5	0.3	nd	73.5	5.7	nd	400
cottage cheese, reduced fat	78	1.4	0.9	5	13.3	3.3	73	380

All amounts given per 100g, unless otherwise stated

	Calories	Total Fat	Saturated Fat	Cholesterol	Protein	Total Sugar	Calcium	Sodium (Salt)
	Kcals	g	g	mg	g	g	mg	mg
cottage cheese, very low fat, onion and cheddar (Asda)	94	3.1	nd	nd	13	nd	nd	nd
cream cheese	439	47.4	29.7	95	3.1	Trace	98	300
dairy spread with cheese, low fat (Asda)	185	9	nd	nd	18	nd	nd	nd
Danish blue	347	29.6	18.5	75	20.1	Trace	500	1260
double Gloucester (Tesco)	404	34	22.5	nd	24.4	0.1	nd	590
Edam	333	25.4	15.9	80	26	Trace	770	1020
feta	250	20.2	13.7	70	15.6	1.5	360	1440
fromage frais, plain	113	7.1	4.4	25	6.8	5.7	89	31
very low fat	58	0.2	0.1	1	7.7	6.8	87	33
Gorgonzola (Tesco)	386	34	22.5	nd	20	nd	600	nd
Gouda	375	31	19.4	100	24	Trace	740	910
Gruyère	412	32.3	18.9	109	29.8	0	1010	335
hard cheese, red fat, (Heinz)	297	21	13.2	nd	27	0	nd	700
Lancashire Farmhouse (Tesco)	373	31	19.4	nd	23.3	0.1	nd	700
Lyneswold	425	40.3	25.2	115	15.6	Trace	270	560
mozzarella	293	22.5	13.7	81	20.2	nd	538	388
mozzarella (M&S)	268	20	13.2	nd	18	2	nd	400
Parmesan	452	32.7	20.5	100	39.4	Trace	600	1320
grated parmesan (M&S)	408	29.7	18.1	nd	35.1	0.1	nd	800

All amounts given per 100g, unless otherwise stated

43

Milk and Dairy

Milk and Dairy

	Calories	Total Fat	Saturated Fat	Cholesterol	Protein	Total Sugars	Calcium	Sodium (Salt)
	Kcals	g	g	mg	g	g	mg	mg
Provolone	352	26.6	17	70	25.5	nd	754	873
Quark	69	0.3	0	0	14	nd	33	14
ricotta	174	13	8.3	50	11.3	1.5	207	84
Roquefort	370	30.6	19.2	92	21.5	nd	662	1806
roule, herb and garlic	329	31	21.1	nd	10	2.5	nd	1.5
cheese slices, red fat, (Heinz)	197	10	6.1	nd	26.5	0.2	nd	700
Stilton	411	35.5	22.2	105	22.7	0.1	320	930
soft cheese, full fat	313	31	19.4	90	8.6	Trace	110	330
soft cheese, medium fat	179	14.5	9.1	42	9.2	3.1	nd	nd
Coffee whitener (Asda)	567	38.5	38	nd	2.9	9.8	nd	100
lite (Asda)	448	16.9	16.1	nd	3.2	14.4	nd	800
Condensed milk	333	10.1	6.3	36	8.5	55.5	290	140
Cream, aerosol (M&S)	320	7.9	5	nd	0.4	1.3	nd	0
extra thick double (M&S)	445	47.5	29.7	nd	1.7	2.6	nd	30
single	198	19.1	11.9	55	2.6	4.1	91	49
soured	205	19.9	12.5	60	2.9	3.8	93	41
whipping	373	39.3	24.6	105	2	3.1	62	40
double	449	48	30	130	1.7	2.7	50	37
clotted	586	63.5	39.7	170	1.6	2.3	37	18
canned spray	239	23.9	14.9	65	2.5	3.7	86	53

All amounts given per 100g, unless otherwise stated

	Calories	Total Fat	Saturated Fat	Cholesterol	Protein	Total Sugar	Calcium	Sodium (Salt)
	Kcals	g	g	mg	g	g	mg	mg
Crème fraîche (M&S)	379	40	26.5	nd	1.9	1.4	nd	0
Dried skimmed milk	348	0.6	0.4	12	36.1	52.9	1280	550
Ducks' eggs, boiled	183	13.6	3.7	890	13.7	nd	66	107
Eggs, chicken, boiled	147	10.8	3.1	385	12.5	Trace	57	140
fried	179	13.9	4	435	13.6	Trace	65	160
poached	147	10.8	3.1	385	12.5	Trace	57	140
scrambled, with milk	247	22.6	11.6	350	10.7	0.6	63	1030
white only	1450	0	0	0	301	nd	147	78
yolk only	354	31	5.2	735	15	nd	147	78
Evaporated milk	151	9.4	5.9	34	8.4	8.5	290	180
Goats' milk	60	3.5	2.3	10	3.1	4.4	100	42
Milk, pasteurised, whole	66	3.9	2.4	14	3.2	4.8	115	55
Carnation (Nestlé)	160	9	5.7	nd	8.2	11.5	280	180
Coffeemate (Nestlé)	551	34.8	34.1	nd	2.4	57	nd	200
semi-skimmed	46	1.6	1	7	3.3	120	120	55
skimmed	33	0.1	0.1	2	3.3	5	120	55
spray dried, skimmed	36	0.1	0.1	nd	nd	nd	nd	100
sterilised, whole	66	3.9	2.4	14	3.5	4.5	120	57
vitamin enriched (M&S)	48	1.7	1	nd	3.7	4.7	nd	60
Rennet	168	12.7	0	14	9.2	1.5	130	107

All amounts given per 100g, unless otherwise stated

Milk and Dairy

Milk and Dairy

	Calories	Total Fat	Saturated Fat	Cholesterol	Protein	Total Sugars	Calcium	Sodium (Salt)
	Kcals	g	g	mg	g	g	mg	mg
Yogurt, plain	79	3	1.7	11	5.7	7.8	200	80
Bio (M&S)	91	3.5	2.2	nd	6.3	8.6	nd	90
fromage frais lite (M&S)	59	0.1	0	nd	9.8	4.8	nd	0
fruit	79	3	1.7	11	5.7	7.8	200	80
lite black cherry (M&S)	45	0.1	0	nd	4.1	5.1	nd	0
lite peach melba (M&S)	44	0.1	0	nd	4.2	4.8	nd	0
lite raspberry (M&S)	44	0.1	0	nd	4.2	4.5	nd	0
lite rhubarb (M&S)	42	0.1	0	nd	4.2	4.4	nd	0
low fat bio, toffee (M&S)	101	2.2	1.6	nd	4.7	16.2	nd	70
low fat, plain	105	2.8	1.5	10	5.1	15.7	160	82
low fat, fruit	56	0.8	0.5	4	5.1	7.5	190	83
Greek	90	0.7	0.4	4	4.1	17.9	150	64
Greek honey (M&S)	153	8.3	5.4	nd	4.4	15.6	nd	50
low fat French set, vanilla (Asda)	115	9.1	5.2	nd	6.4	2	150	71
low fat French set, apricot (Asda)	84	1	nd	nd	4.3	nd	nd	nd
very low fat French set, strawberry (Asda)	77	1.2	nd	nd	4	nd	nd	nd
custard style, apricot and nectarine (Asda)	36	0.1	nd	nd	4	nd	nd	nd

All amounts given per 100g, unless otherwise stated

	Calories	Total Fat	Saturated Fat	Cholesterol	Protein	Total Sugar	Calcium	Sodium (Salt)
	Kcals	g	g	mg	g	g	mg	mg
custard style, raspberry and redcurrant (Asda)	131	5.4	nd	nd	4.2	nd	nd	nd
Swiss muesli (M&S)	146	5.6	3.2	nd	6.4	16.6	nd	60

All amounts given per 100g, unless otherwise stated

Milk and Dairy

Meat

MEAT

	Calories	Total Fat	Saturated Fat	Cholesterol	Protein	Iron	Sodium (Salt)	Folic Acid
	Kcals	g	g	mg	g	mg	mg	mcg
Bacon, rasher, back, fried	465	40.6	15.9	143	24.9	1.3	1910	1
British smoked (M&S)	206	15.7	5.5	nd	17.3	nd	1110	nd
British unsmoked (M&S)	174	11.7	4.9	nd	17.2	nd	1150	1
middle, fried	477	42.3	16.5	149	24.1	1.3	1870	nd
reduced salt (M&S)	226	18	7.2	nd	15.9	nd	800	1
streaky, fried	496	44.8	17.5	158	23.1	1.2	1820	1
back, grilled	405	33.8	13.2	125	25.3	1.5	2020	1
middle, grilled	416	35.1	13.8	130	24.9	1.5	2000	1
streaky, grilled	422	36	14.1	133	24.5	1.5	1990	1
lean only, average, grilled	292	18.9	7.4	70	30.5	1.6	2240	2
Beef, corned, canned	217	12.1	6.3	93	26.9	2.9	950	2
burger with onion, grilled, (Sains)	43	2.5	31.3	0.1	3.9	0.2	nd	300
brisket, boiled	326	23.9	9.5	91	27.6	2.8	73	13
mince, stewed	229	15.2	6.5	83	23.1	3.1	320	16
ox tongue (M&S)	277	21.6	10.1	nd	19.1	nd	700	nd
roast (M&S)	130	2.8	1.3	nd	26.3	nd	200	nd
roast slices (Asda)	112	3.6	1.6	nd	18.3	nd	700	nd
beef spread	194	13.7	7.5	nd	13.5	nd	800	nd

All amounts given per 100g, unless otherwise stated

	Calories	Total Fat	Saturated Fat	Cholesterol	Protein	Iron	Sodium (Salt)	Folic Acid
	Kcals	g	g	mg	g	mg	mg	mcg
rump steak, fried	246	14.6	6.2	82	28.6	3.2	54	15
rump steak, grilled	218	12.1	5.2	82	3.4	3.4	55	15
rump steak, lean only, grilled	168	6	2.5	82	28.6	3.5	56	17
steak au poivre (M&S)	169	11	6	nd	17	nd	1600	nd
salted, dried	250	1.5	nd	nd	55.4	4.9	nd	nd
silverside, salted, boiled	242	14.2	6.2	83	28.6	2.8	910	15
sirloin, roast	284	21.1	6.2	83	23.6	1.9	54	14
sirloin, lean only, roast	192	9.1	2	82	27.6	2.1	59	17
stewing steak, stewed	223	11	4.7	82	30.9	3	360	16
topside, roast	214	12	4.1	82	26.6	2.6	48	15
topside, lean only, roast	156	4.4	1.4	82	29.2	2.8	49	17
Black pudding (M&S)	340	24.5	11.1	nd	12.1	nd	1110	nd
Chicken, meat only, boiled	183	7.3	2.4	97	29.2	1.2	82	8
corn fed, breasts baked, (Sains)	181	9.7	2.9	<100	23.5	nd	<100	nd
coronation (M&S)	333	28	4.3	nd	14.1	nd	200	nd
light meat, boiled	163	4.9	1.6	65	29.7	0.6	70	4
dark meat, boiled	204	9.9	3.2	132	28.6	1.9	95	13
meat only, roast	148	5.4	1.6	76	24.8	0.8	81	10
meat and skin, roast	216	14	4.2	103	22.6	0.8	72	nd
half roast (M&S)	217	14.1	4.5	nd	22.2	nd	600	nd

All amounts given per 100g, unless otherwise stated

Meat

49

Meat

	Calories	Total Fat	Saturated Fat	Cholesterol	Protein	Iron	Sodium (Salt)	Folic Acid
	Kcals	g	g	mg	g	mg	mg	mcg
Chicken,								
light meat, roast	142	4	1.2	56	26.5	0.5	71	7
dark meat, roast	155	6.9	2.1	97	23.1	1	91	13
breaded, fried	242	12.7	2.1	36	18	nd	420	nd
southern fried breast (M&S)	186	6.9	1.3	nd	20.6	nd	800	nd
chicken spread	197	13	4	nd	14.7	nd	800	nd
chicken tikka, slices (Asda)	111	1.4	nd	nd	20.5	nd	nd	nd
Duck, meat only, roast	189	9.7	2.7	160	25.3	2.7	96	10
Barbary duck (Sains)	240	17.9	5.9	100	20.2	nd	nd	nd
breast joint (M&S)	305	25.3	8.1	nd	11.4	nd	300	nd
crispy aromatic duck (M&S)	206	14.1	4.7	nd	11.9	nd	300	nd
meat, fat and skin, roast	339	29	7.9	nd	19.6	2.7	76	nd
Farmhouse pâté (M&S)	222	16.3	7.8	nd	15.9	nd	500	nd
Gammon/ham, joint, boiled	269	18.9	7.4	70	24.7	1.3	960	Trace
joint, lean only, boiled	167	5.5	2.1	20	29.4	1.5	1110	1
rasher, grilled	228	12.2	4.8	45	29.5	1.4	2140	2
canned	120	5.1	1.9	68	18.4	1.2	1250	Trace
honey roast slices (M&S)	109	2.2	0.8	nd	19.5	nd	100	nd
smoked, sliced (Asda)	95	2.3	nd	nd	17.4	nd	nd	nd
Parma ham (Tesco)	207	9.45	3.2	nd	30.4	nd	1900	nd

All amounts given per 100g, unless otherwise stated

	Calories	Total Fat	Saturated Fat	Cholesterol	Protein	Iron	Sodium (Salt)	Folic Acid
	Kcals	g	g	mg	g	mg	mg	mcg
Grouse, meat only, roast	173	5.3	1.2	nd	31.3	7.6	96	37
Haggis (M&S)	253	16.9	8	nd	13.8	nd	nd	nd
Kidney, lamb, fried	155	6.3	2.1	610	24.6	12	270	79
pig, stewed	153	6.1	2	700	24.4	6.4	370	43
ox, stewed	172	7.7	3.2	690	25.6	8	400	75
Lamb, breast, roast	410	37.1	18.4	106	19.1	1.5	73	3
breast, lean only, roast	252	16.6	7.9	110	25.6	1.7	86	4
chops, grilled	355	29	14.4	107	23.5	1.9	72	3
chops, lean only, grilled	222	12.3	5.9	110	27.8	2.1	75	4
Cutlets, grilled	370	30.9	15.3	107	23	1.9	71	3
cutlets, lean only, grilled	222	12.3	5.9	110	27.8	2.1	75	4
leg, roast	266	17.9	8.9	108	26.1	2.5	65	3
leg, lean only, roast	191	8.1	3.9	110	29.4	2.7	67	4
leg with mint gravy (M&S)	133	8	4.7	nd	14.2	nd	200	nd
scrag and neck, stewed	292	21.1	10.5	108	25.6	2.2	240	4
shoulder, roast	316	26.3	13.1	107	19.9	1.6	61	3
shoulder, lean only, roast	196	11.2	5.4	110	23.8	1.8	65	4
Liver, calf, fried	254	13.2	4	330	26.9	7.5	170	320
chicken, fried	194	10.9	3.4	350	20.7	9.1	240	500
lamb, fried	232	14	4	400	22.9	10	190	240

All amounts given per 100g, unless otherwise stated

Meat

Meat

	Calories	Total Fat	Saturated Fat	Cholesterol	Protein	Iron	Sodium (Salt)	Folic Acid
	Kcals	g	g	mg	g	mg	mg	mcg
Liver,								
ox, stewed	198	9.5	3.5	240	24.8	7.8	110	290
pig, stewed	189	8.1	2.5	290	25.6	17	130	110
Partridge, meat only, roast	212	7.2	1.9	nd	36.7	7.7	100	nd
Pheasant, meat only, roast	213	9.3	3.1	nd	32.2	8.4	100	nd
Pork, belly rashers, grilled	398	34.8	12.9	105	21.1	1	95	4
chops, loin, grilled	332	24.2	9	108	28.5	1.2	84	6
chops, loin, lean only, grilled	226	10.7	3.8	110	32.3	1.2	84	7
leg, roast	286	19.8	7.3	107	26.9	1.3	79	6
leg, lean only, roast	185	6.9	2.4	110	30.7	1.3	79	7
pork and egg pie (M&S)	326	24	10.4	nd	10.6	nd	500	nd
pressed pork tongue (M&S)	156	9.9	3.7	nd	14.9	nd	1300	nd
peppered salami (M&S)	436	36.8	23.5	nd	20.4	nd	2600	nd
sausagemeat (Asda)	301	23.5	nd	nd	11.8	nd	nd	nd
free range sausages (M&S)	297	24.2	9	nd	13.4	nd	400	nd
pork/beef sausages (M&S)	295	23.8	10.2	nd	11.5	nd	900	nd
reduced fat sausages (M&S)	196	12.3	4.4	nd	10.8	nd	500	nd
tomato sausages (M&S)	274	21	8.9	nd	13.3	nd	800	nd
Rabbit, meat only, stewed	179	7.7	3.2	137	27.3	1.9	32	4

All amounts given per 100g, unless otherwise stated

	Calories	Total Fat	Saturated Fat	Cholesterol	Protein	Iron	Sodium (Salt)	Folic Acid
	Kcals	g	g	mg	g	mg	mg	mcg
Tongue, ox, boiled	293	23.9	nd	100	19.5	3	1000	5
sheep, stewed	289	24	nd	270	18.2	3.4	80	4
Tripe, dressed, stewed	100	4.5	2.4	160	14.8	0.7	73	1
Turkey, meat only, roast	140	2.7	0.9	79	28.8	0.9	57	15
meat and skin, roast	171	6.5	2.1	191	28	0.9	52	nd
light meat, roast	132	1.4	0.4	62	29.8	0.5	45	13
dark meat, roast	148	4.1	1.3	100	27.8	1.4	71	17
roast breast (M&S)	126	2.7	0.8	nd	25.3	nd	400	nd
smoked breast slices (Asda)	105	2.1	1	nd	20.2	nd	600	nd
smoked (M&S)	102	1.4	0.5	nd	18.4	nd	1110	nd
Veal, cutlet, fried	215	8.1	0.8	109	31.4	1.6	110	4
fillet, roast	230	11.5	3.7	155	31.6	1.6	97	6
Venison, roast	198	6.4	nd	nd	35	7.8	86	

All amounts given per 100g, unless otherwise stated

53

Meat

FOOD FACTS

	Calories	Total Fat	Saturated Fat	Cholesterol	Protein	Calcium	Selenium	Sodium (Salt)
	Kcals	g	g	mg	g	mg	mcg	mg
FISH AND SEAFOOD								
Anchovies, canned in oil, drained	280	19.9	nd	nd	25.2	300	4.1	3930
Carp, baked	162	7.2	1.4	84	22.9	52	nd	63
Caviar	252	3	4.1	588	24.6	275	0.1	1500
caviar (M&S)	253	28.5	16.5	nd	30.5	nd	nd	1133
Clams, boiled	148	1.9	0.2	67	25.5	92	nd	112
Cod fillets, poached	94	1.1	0.4	60	20.9	29	33	110
cod & chips (M&S)	144	5.5	0.6	nd	7.8	nd	nd	300
baked	96	1.2	0.5	48	21.4	22	34	340
in batter, fried	199	10.3	0.9	nd	19.6	80	nd	100
in crumbs (M&S)	158	6.1	0.8	nd	15.1	nd	nd	300
grilled	95	1.3	0.5	60	20.8	10	33	91
leek cod toppers (M&S)	94	3.7	2.1	nd	11.3	nd	nd	260
cod's roe, fried	202	11.9	1.2	500	20.9	17	nd	130
Cockles, boiled	48	0.3	0.1	52	11.3	130	45	3520
Crab, boiled	127	5.2	0.7	72	20.1	29	17	370
canned	81	0.9	0.1	72	18.1	120	nd	550
paste (Asda)	152	7.9	nd	nd	14.4	nd	nd	nd
pâté (M&S)	183	14	5.4	nd	13.7	nd	nd	600

All amounts given per 100g, unless otherwise stated

	Calories	Total Fat	Saturated Fat	Cholesterol	Protein	Calcium	Selenium	Sodium (Salt)
	Kcals	g	g	mg	g	mg	mcg	mg
Crayfish, boiled	87	1.3	0.2	138	17.6	51	nd	98
Dogfish, in batter, fried	265	18.8	1.6	nd	16.7	42	nd	290
Eel, baked	237	14.9	3	161	23.7	26	0.1	65
Fish casserole (M&S)	470	7.4	4.5	nd	6.2	nd	nd	300
Gravadlax (M&S)	198	13.1	4.1	nd	16	nd	nd	1150
Haddock, steamed	98	0.8	0.2	48	22.8	55	30	120
in batter	233	14.3	2.5	nd	11.6	nd	nd	400
in crumbs, fried	174	8.3	0.7	nd	21.4	110	30	180
smoked, steamed	101	0.9	0.2	54	23.3	58	30	1220
Halibut, steamed	131	4	0.5	60	23.8	13	nd	110
Herring, grilled	199	13	3.7	50	20.4	33	41	170
fried	234	15.1	4.3	80	23.1	39	46	100
rollmops (M&S)	159	6.4	3.8	nd	10	nd	nd	700
Kipper, baked	205	11.4	1.8	38	25.5	65	43	990
Lemon sole, steamed	91	0.9	0.1	60	20.6	21	44	120
in crumbs, fried	216	13	1.3	nd	16.1	95	nd	140
Lobster, boiled	119	3.4	nd	150	22.1	62	nd	330
Mackerel, fried	188	11.3	2.3	62	21.5	28	34	150
smoked	354	30.9	6.3	104	18.9	20	27	750
Monkfish, steamed	76	1.5	0.2	25	14.5	8	nd	18

All amounts given per 100g, unless otherwise stated

Fish and Seafood

Fish and Seafood

	Calories	Total Fat	Saturated Fat	Cholesterol	Protein	Calcium	Selenium	Sodium (Salt)
	Kcals	g	g	mg	g	mg	mcg	mg
Mussels, boiled	87	2	0.4	58	17.2	200	45	210
Oysters	59	1.6	0.4	26	5.2	nd	nd	178
Perch, baked	117	1.2	0.2	115	24.8	102	Trace	79
Pilchards, canned in tomato sauce	126	5.4	1.1	56	18.8	300	2.7	370
Plaice, steamed	93	1.9	0.3	50	18.9	38	38	120
filled plaice (M&S)	171	10	2	nd	9.3	nd	nd	400
in batter, fried	279	18	1.5	nd	15.8	93	nd	220
in crumbs, fried	228	13.7	1.4	nd	18	67	38	220
Prawns, boiled	119	3.4	0.4	81	22.1	150	18	1590
chinese prawns (M&S)	198	8.4	1.3	nd	10.3	nd	nd	700
cocktail (M&S)	372	36	3	nd	9.2	nd	nd	500
large peeled prawns (M&S)	95	1.6	0	nd	20	nd	nd	600
Salmon, steamed	197	13	2.4	55	20.1	29	0.8	110
canned	155	8.2	1.5	34	20.3	93	1.4	570
smoked	142	4.5	0.8	50	25.4	19	0.6	1880
Irish smoked salmon (M&S)	158	6.5	3	nd	23.4	nd	nd	700
smoked salmon pâté (M&S)	258	22	12.6	nd	14	nd	nd	600
salmon & shrimp paste	122	6	nd	nd	15	nd	nd	nd
salmon spread	134	5.8	2.1	nd	14.8	nd	nd	500
Sardines, canned in oil, drained	217	13.6	2.8	65	23.7	550	2.9	650

All amounts given per 100g, unless otherwise stated

	Calories	Total Fat	Saturated Fat	Cholesterol	Protein	Calcium	Selenium	Sodium (Salt)
	Kcals	g	g	mg	g	mg	mcg	mg
canned in tomato sauce	177	11.6	3.3	76	17.8	460	4.6	700
sardine & tomato paste	161	9.9	nd	nd	14.7	nd	nd	nd
Scampi, in breadcrumbs, fried	316	17.6	1.7	110	12.2	99	15	380
scampi in crumbs (M&S)	199	10.2	1.5	nd	11.4	nd	nd	nd
Sea bass, baked	124	2.6	0.7	53	23.7	13	nd	87
Seafood pasta (M&S)	103	5	3.1	nd	7.4	nd	nd	400
Shrimps, canned, drained	94	1.2	0.2	200	20.8	110	52	980
in batter, fried	199	12.1	1.2	nd	17.9	50	nd	140
Squid, fried	175	7.5	1.9	260	18	39	nd	306
Swordfish, baked	155	5.1	1.4	51	25.4	6	nd	115
Trout, steamed	135	4.5	1	97	23.5	36	1	88
Rainbow trout (M&S)	123	4.7	2.4	nd	21.7	nd	nd	nd
Tuna, canned in oil, drained	189	9	1.4	50	27.1	12	1.6	290
canned in brine, drained	99	0.6	0.2	51	23.5	8	1	320
tuna in spring water (M&S)	117	0.5	0.1	nd	25	nd	nd	1120
tuna & mayonnaise spread	238	18.4	3.1	nd	17	nd	nd	500
Whelks, steamed	274	0.8	0.1	129	47.7	113	nd	412
Whitebait, fried	525	47.5	4.4	nd	19.5	860	5.1	230
Whiting, steamed	92	0.9	0.1	46	20.9	42	22	130
in crumbs, fried	191	10.3	1	nd	18.1	48	nd	200

All amounts given per 100g, unless otherwise stated

Fish and Seafood

Fats and Oils

FOOD FACTS

All amounts given per 100g, unless otherwise stated

FATS AND OILS

	Calories	Total Fat	Saturated Fat	Monosaturated Fat	Polyunsaturated Fat	Cholesterol	Vitamin A	Vitamin E
	Kcals	g	g	g	g	mg	mcg	mg
Butter	737	81.7	54	19.8	2.6	230	815	2
unsalted English (M&S)	755	83.7	54.7	nd	nd	nd	nd	nd
Dripping	891	99	54.8	36.7	2.5	94	nd	0.3
Ghee butter	898	99.8	66	24.1	3.4	280	675	3.31
Lard	891	99	40.8	9.6	9.6	93	Trace	Trace
Low-fat Spread	390	40.5	11.2	17.6	9.9	6	920	6.33
Margarine, average	739	81.6	nd	nd	nd	nd	780	8
hard, animal and vegetable fat	739	81.6	30.4	36.5	10.8	285	665	nd
hard, vegetable fat only	739	81.6	35.9	33	9.4	15	665	nd
olive (M&S)	545	60	13.2	nd	nd	15	nd	nd
soft, animal and vegetable fat	739	81.6	26.9	37.2	13.8	225	860	nd
soft, vegetable fat only	739	81.6	25	31	21.8	9	860	nd
half fat sunflower (M&S)	378	40	7.3	nd	nd	nd	nd	nd
polyunsaturated	739	81.6	16.2	20.6	41.4	7	775	nd
Suet, shredded	826	86.7	48	32.1	2.1	82	52	1.5
Vegetable oil, blended	899	99.9	10.4	35.5	48.2	0	0	nd
almond	883	99.9	8.1	69.9	17.7	nd	nd	nd
avocado	884	99.9	11.6	70.6	13.5	0	0	nd

Vegetable oil,	Calories	Total Fat	Saturated Fat	Monosaturated Fat	Polyunsaturated Fat	Cholesterol	Vitamin A	Vitamin E
	Kcals	g	g	g	g	mg	mcg	mg
coconut	899	99.9	85.2	6.6	1.7	0	0	0.66
corn	899	99.9	12.7	24.7	57.8	0	0	17.24
grapeseed	884	99.9	9.6	16.2	69.7	0	0	nd
hazelnut	884	99.9	7.4	78	10.1	0	0	nd
olive	899	99.9	14	69.7	11.2	0	0	5.1
palm	883	99.9	49.3	36.8	17.7	nd	nd	nd
peanut / groundnut	899	99.9	18.8	47.8	28.5	0	0	15.16
rapeseed	899	99.9	6.6	57.2	31.5	0	0	22.21
safflower	899	99.9	10.2	12.6	72.1	0	0	40.68
sesame	881	99.7	14.2	37.3	43.9	0	0	nd
soya	899	99.9	14.5	23.2	56.5	0	0	16.29
sunflower	899	99.9	11.9	20.2	63	0	0	49.22
walnut	884	99.9	9.1	22.8	63.3	0	0	32.1
wheatgerm	899	99.9	18.8	15.9	60.7	0	0	136.65

All amounts given per 100g, unless otherwise stated

Fats and Oils

Nuts and Seeds

(Kernel only)	Calories	Total Fat	Saturated Fat	Protein	Calcium	Iron	Zinc	Vitamin E
	Kcals	g	g	g	mg	mg	mg	mg
NUTS AND SEEDS (Kernel only)								
Almonds	612	55.8	4.7	21.1	240	3	3.2	23.98
Brazils	682	68.2	16.4	14.1	170	2.5	4.2	7.18
Cashew nuts	580	1.5	29.7	1.1	19	1.4	1.1	nd
Chestnuts	170	2.7	0.5	2	46	0.9	0.5	1.2
Coconut	38.2	1.5	29.7	1.1	19	1.4	1.1	nd
desiccated	604	62	53.4	5.6	23	3.6	0.9	1.26
Hazelnuts	650	63.5	4.7	14.1	140	3.2	2.1	24.98
Macadamia nuts	748	77.6	11.2	7.9	47	1.6	1.1	1.49
Marzipan (almond paste)	404	14.4	1.2	5.3	66	0.9	0.8	6.18
Monkey nuts, shelled (Sains)	626	52.6	9.3	29.9	nd	nd	nd	nd
Peanut butter, smooth	623	53.7	11.7	22.6	37	2.1	3	4.99
Peanuts	564	46.1	8.2	25.6	60	2.5	3.5	10.09
salted	581	49.3	6.8	26.3	88	7.7	4.7	11.7
dry roasted	586	50	6.9	23.7	54	2.3	3.3	nd
Pecan nuts	689	70.1	5.7	9.2	61	2.2	5.3	4.34
Pine nuts	688	68.6	4.6	14	11	5.6	6.5	13.65
Pistachio nuts	577	48	6.1	20.6	135	6.8	1.3	nd
Poppy seeds	nd	44	nd	20.6	1580	11.1	8.5	2.72

All amounts given per 100g, unless otherwise stated

	Calories	Total Fat	Saturated Fat	Protein	Calcium	Iron	Zinc	Vitamin E
	Kcals	g	g	g	mg	mg	mg	mg
Pumpkin seeds	542	54.9	8.7	25.5	45.1	9.9	7.5	nd
Sesame seeds	598	58	8.3	18.2	670	10.4	5.3	2.53
Sunflower seeds	581	47.5	4.5	19.8	110	6.4	5.1	37.77
Tahini paste (sesame)	607	58.9	8.4	18.5	680	10.6	5.4	2.57
Walnuts	688	68.5	5.6	14.7	94	2.9	2.7	3.83

(Kernel only)

All amounts given per 100g, unless otherwise stated

Nuts and Seeds

Herbs and Spices

(dried unless stated)	Calories Kcals	Calcium mg	Iron mg	Zinc mg	Beta-carotene mcg	Vitamin C mg	Folic Acid mcg
HERBS AND SPICES							
Allspice, ground	nd	660	7.1	1	325	0	0
Anise seeds	nd	650	37	5.3	nd	0	0
Basil	251	2110	42	5.8	5630	0	0
fresh	40	250	5.5	0.7	3950	26	nd
Bay leaves, dried	313	830	43	3.7	3710	0	0
Black pepper	nd	430	11.2	1.4	115	0	0
Caraway seeds	nd	950	32.3	5.2	215	0	0
Cardamon	nd	130	100	2.6	Trace	0	0
Cayenne pepper	318	150	34.1	2	36810	0	0
Chervil	237	1350	31.9	8.8	nd	0	16.9
Chilli peppers	250	250	15	2.7	3413	0	0
powder	nd	280	14.3	2.7	21000	0	0
Chinese 5 spice	nd	1040	25.6	2.9	138	0	nd
Chives	500	1000	20	nd	nd	650	nd
fresh	23	85	1.6	0.4	2300	45	nd
Cinnamon, ground	nd	1230	38.1	2	155	0	0
Cloves	nd	730	5.6	2.2	320	0	0

All amounts given per 100g, unless otherwise stated

(dried unless stated)	Calories	Calcium	Iron	Zinc	Beta-carotene	Vitamin C	Folic Acid
	Kcals	mg	mg	mg	mcg	mg	mcg
Coriander leaves	279	1250	8	2.9	7870	0	0
fresh	20	98	1.9	0.2	610	63	18
Coriander seeds	nd	660	8	4.7	Trace	0	0
Cumin	nd	970	69	4.2	760	0	0
Curry powder	233	820	5.1	nd	100	0	0
Dill	253	1780	48.8	3.3	33260	0	0
fresh	25	750	3.2	1.8	6100	86	36
Dill seeds	nd	1520	16.3	4.5	32	0	0
Fennel	nd	1200	12.3	3.7	81	0	0
Garlic powder	246	65	3.9	2.6	Trace	0	0
Ginger, ground	258	97	46.8	4.7	220	0	nd
fresh	49	17	0.6	0.4	35	4	nd
Horseradish	237	377	3.8	nd	nd	221	0
Liquorice powder	nd	580	49.8	nd	nd	0	0
Mace, ground	nd	250	13.9	2.3	480	0	0
Marjoram	271	1990	82.7	3.6	4840	0	0
Mint	279	1370	nd	nd	4830	Trace	nd
fresh	43	210	9.5	nd	740	31	110
Mustard powder	452	330	9.5	6.5	nd	0	0
Nutmeg, ground	nd	180	3	2.2	60	0	0

All amounts given per 100g, unless otherwise stated

Herbs and Spices

Herbs and Spices

(dried unless stated)	Calories	Calcium	Iron	Zinc	Beta-carotene	Vitamin C	Folic Acid
	Kcals	mg	mg	mg	mcg	mg	mcg
Nutmeg, fresh	512	24	0.4	nd	41.9	0	nd
Oregano	306	1580	44	4.4	4140	0	0
fresh	66	310	nd	0.9	810	45	nd
Paprika	289	180	23.6	4.1	36250	0	0
Parsley	181	1080	41.5	3.8	21750	120	nd
fresh	34	200	7.7	3.8	4040	190	170
Rosemary	331	1280	29.3	3.2	1880	0	0
fresh	99	370	8.5	0.9	550	29	nd
Saffron	310	110	11.1	nd	nd	0	0
Sage	315	1650	28.1	4.7	3540	0	0
fresh	119	600	nd	1.7	1290	Trace	nd
Tarragon	295	1140	32.3	3.9	2520	0	0
fresh	49	450	nd	0.6	375	0	0
Thyme	276	1890	nd	2.1	2280	0	0
fresh	95	630	nd	2.1	760	0	0
Turmeric	nd	170	39.5	3.2	15	0	0

All amounts given per 100g, unless otherwise stated

Egg Dishes

	Calories	Total Fat	Saturated Fat	Fibre	Protein	Total Sugars	Iron	Sodium (Salt)
	kcals	g	g	g	g	g	mg	mg
Omelette, plain	191	16.4	7.4	0	10.9	Trace	1.7	1030
cheese	266	22.6	12.2	0	15.9	Trace	1.2	900
Quiche, cheese and egg	314	22.2	10.3	0.6	12.5	1.6	1	120
cheese and egg, wholemeal	308	22.4	10.4	0.9	13.2	1.7	1.4	340
cheese and onion (Asda)	304	19.8	9.1	0.2	10.3	9.1	nd	965
chicken and courgette (Asda)	273	17.8	nd	nd	11.1	nd	nd	nd
tuna, sweetcorn and broccoli (Asda)	254	16.2	nd	nd	10	nd	nd	nd
Scotch eggs	251	17.1	4.3	nd	12	Trace	1.8	670

Fish Dishes

	Calories	Total Fat	Saturated Fat	Fibre	Protein	Total Sugars	Iron	Sodium (Salt)
	kcals	g	g	g	g	g	mg	mg
Atlantic pie (M&S)	109	5.1	2.8	1.6	7.8	3.5	nd	300
Calamari in crispy batter (Sains)	320	21.6	3.1	2.5	21.6	0.3	nd	nd
Cod steaks in butter sauce (Walls)	109	5.4	3.2	0.1	10	2.3	nd	400
in parsley sauce (Walls)	170	5.5	2.2	0.2	19	5.1	nd	500
crisp crumb (Walls)	217	13.2	6.6	0.8	12.7	0.8	nd	500
Fish cakes, fried	188	10.5	1	17	9.1	Trace	1	500
salmon in wholemeal breadcrumbs (Walls)	185	9.8	4.5	1	9.1	0.5	nd	700
value (Walls)	112	0.4	0.1	0.5	9.4	0.5	nd	500

All amounts given per 100g, unless otherwise stated

Savoury Dishes

Savoury Dishes

FOOD FACTS

	Calories	Total Fat	Saturated Fat	Fibre	Protein	Total Sugars	Iron	Sodium (Salt)
	kcals	g	g	g	g	g	mg	mg
Fish fingers, grilled	214	9	2.8	35	15.1	Trace	0.8	380
fried	233	12.7	2.8	nd	13.5	Trace	0.7	350
fishfingers (M&S)	196	9.5	2	0.3	12.3	0	nd	500
cod fillet (Walls)	159	6.9	3.5	0.5	11.4	0.4	nd	400
Fish paste	169	10.4	nd	nd	15.3	Trace	9	600
Fish pie	105	3	1.2	19	8	1.5	0.4	250
Hake in parsley sauce (M&S)	199	14.3	2.5	0.5	11.6	2	nd	400
Kedgeree	166	7.9	2.3	116	14.2	0.1	0.8	870
Pasta & Tuna bake (M&S)	132	6.8	4.2	0.4	8.4	0.6	nd	300
Prawn balls (M&S)	264	14.1	0.7	1	10.8	1.8	nd	400
Prawn Biryani (M&S)	170	5.7	1.8	1.2	7.1	1.6	nd	300
Prawn toasts (M&S)	347	27.7	6.1	1.4	12	1.1	nd	600
Salmon watercress sauce (M&S)	151	10	5.3	0.7	12	2.8	nd	200
Salmon & asparagus with tagliatelle (Findus Lean Cuisine)	100	2.8	0.7	0.6	6.3	2.7	nd	200
Taramasalata	446	46.4	3.2	37	3.2	Trace	0.4	650
Tuna fishcakes (M&S)	244	14.8	3.8	1	10.8	0.4	nd	1110

All amounts given per 100g, unless otherwise stated

GRAIN DISHES

	Calories	Total Fat	Saturated Fat	Fibre	Protein	Total Sugars	Iron	Sodium (Salt)
	kcals	g	g	g	g	g	mg	mg
Cannelloni (M&S)	136	6.8	3.2	0.9	7.8	1.6	nd	300
Dumplings	208	11.7	6.4	0.9	2.8	0.4	0.6	400
Egg fried rice (M&S)	136	5.5	1	0.5	3.9	0.1	nd	120
Golden veg rice (Walls)	103	0.3	0.1	1.4	3.4	2.4	nd	500
Macaroni cheese	178	10.8	5.6	0.5	7.3	2.9	0.4	310
Menu Master (Walls)	127	6.8	3.4	0.4	5.7	1.9	nd	400
Macaroni cheese bake (M&S)	169	8.7	4.9	0.3	7.8	0.7	nd	600
Original veg rice (Walls)	114	0.5	0.1	2.2	4.2	1.8	nd	500
Pilau rice (M&S)	170	3.9	1.3	1.1	3.6	1.1	nd	300
Pizza, cheese and tomato	235	11.8	5.5	1.5	9	2.2	1	570
American hot, deep, (M&S)	282	16.4	8.4	0.8	14.4	1.3	nd	600
bacon & mushroom, deep pan, (M&S)	239	12.8	6.1	0.9	13	1.2	nd	500
thin base cheese and tomato (M&S)	222	10.6	5.4	1.2	19.7	2.6	nd	600
pizza bases (Asda)	257	0.6	nd	nd	8.4	nd	nd	nd
ham and mushroom (Asda)	220	4.8	nd	nd	11.4	nd	nd	nd
deep pan, cheese and tomato (Asda)	255	6.4	3.5	1.9	10.7	1.5	nd	500
Italian Margherita (M&S)	263	14.4	3.7	1.4	8.7	4.4	nd	400
lite vegetable (M&S)	112	3	0.8	1.6	6.6	3.3	nd	300

All amounts given per 100g, unless otherwise stated

Savoury Dishes

Savoury Dishes

	Calories	Total Fat	Saturated Fat	Fibre	Protein	Total Sugars	Iron	Sodium (Salt)
	kcals	g	g	g	g	g	mg	mg
Quiche, tomato & cheese (M&S)	260	18.1	8.2	0.9	8.7	2.4	nd	400
quiche lorraine (M&S)	293	22	10.1	3	13.6	1.1	nd	300
Ravioli, canned in tomato sauce	70	2.2	0.8	0.9	3	2.2	0.8	490
Risotto, plain	224	9.3	2.8	0.4	3	1.2	0.3	410
vegetable (Heinz)	91	1.6	0.3	1.1	2.7	1.7	0.7	200
Spaghetti, canned in tomato sauce	64	0.4	0.1	0.7	1.9	5.5	0.3	420
low sugar & salt (Asda)	56.5	0.1	0	0.5	12.1??	3.1	nd	100
Tagliatelle (M&S)	141	7.1	4.1	0.8	8.5	1	nd	300
Family (M&S)	144	7.8	3.9	0.8	6.5	1.3	nd	300
Yorkshire pudding	208	9.9	5.3	0.9	6.6	3.7	0.9	590
M&S	206	10.7	2.1	1	7	2.5	nd	300
MEAT DISHES								
Baked beans with bacon (Heinz)	91	1.7	0.6	3	6	5.4	1.4	500
beans with burgerbites (Heinz)	103	3.1	1.2	3.1	5.8	4.7	1.4	400
beans with hotdogs (Heinz)	110	5	0.2	2.7	5	3.7	1.4	500
beans with mini sausages (Heinz)	117	4.5	1.7	3.2	5.7	4.3	1.4	700
beans with pepperoni (Heinz)	93	1.9	0.7	3.6	5.5	4.4	1.6	400
beans with pork sausages (Heinz)	109	4.3	1.6	2.7	5	4.8	1.2	700

All amounts given per 100g, unless otherwise stated

	Calories	Total Fat	Saturated Fat	Fibre	Protein	Total Sugars	Iron	Sodium (Salt)
	kcals	g	g	g	g	g	mg	mg
Beefburgers, fried	264	17.3	8	nd	20.4	1.4	3.1	880
economy (Walls)	292	22.4	9.3	0.4	12.6	0.7	nd	700
low fat (Walls)	187	11.3	4.8	0.2	17.6	0.7	nd	500
original burger (Walls)	288	23.8	10	0.2	15	0.7	nd	500
100% beef (Walls)	332	29.7	12.5	0	16.2	Trace	nd	300
Roast beef in gravy, MM (Walls)	77	1.7	0.7	Trace	13.2	0.3	nd	400
Beefsteak pies	280	18.1	10	2.7	9.1	1.3	nd	500
Beef Bourguignon (Tesco)	95	3.8	1.2	0	9.1	1.6	nd	400
Beef grillsteaks (Walls)	312	27	11.3	0	15.9	0.7	nd	nd
Beef Goulash (M&S)	106	3.5	0.3	nd	nd	0	nd	nd
Minced beef/veg, gravy & potato, MM (Walls)	106	5	2.5	0.9	5.1	1.4	nd	400
Beef stew and dumpling, MM, (Walls)	110	3.6	1.5	0.9	7.8	1.7	nd	500
Bolognese sauce	145	11.1	3.1	1	8	3.3	1.4	430
spag bologne (M&S)	110	3.3	1	1.5	7.4	2.7	nd	500
spag Bologne, Menu Master, (Walls)	126	4.1	1.1	1.1	6	2.4	nd	300
Brawn	153	11.5	nd	0	12.4	0	1	750
Cannelloni (M&S)	130	6.6	3	1.4	7.4	3	nd	400
Chicken breast in Gravy, MM, (Walls)	100	3.5	1.2	Trace	14.4	0.1	nd	300
Chicken burgers (Walls)	270	16.7	6.5	0.6	12.9	0.5	nd	500

All amounts given per 100g, unless otherwise stated

Savoury Dishes

Savoury Dishes

	Calories	Total Fat	Saturated Fat	Fibre	Protein	Total Sugars	Iron	Sodium (Salt)
	kcals	g	g	g	g	g	mg	mg
Crispy chicken (Walls)	230	13.8	5.2	0.2	16.2	0.8	nd	400
Chicken goujons (M&S)	264	15	5.4	0.6	15.3	0.2	nd	200
Chicken & broccoli Lasagne, Healthy Options (Walls)	90	2.7	0.8	0.9	6.8	3.3	nd	400
Chicken à l'Orange (Findus Lean Cuisine)	106	1.8	0.6	0.8	9	3.3	nd	200
Chicken and ham pie, individual (Asda)	305	19	nd	nd	9.2	nd	nd	nd
Chicken Kiev (M&S)	245	15.9	6.8	0.4	14.5	0.8	nd	300
Chicken and mush pie (M&S)	106	5.9	2.3	0.4	11.4	1	nd	1170
Chicken & mush casserole, MM (Walls)	93	4.5	1.6	0.3	10.3	0.5	nd	400
Chicken savoury rice (Asda)	116	0.7	0.2	0.4	2.9	0.3	nd	400
Chicken/tarragon sauce (M&S)	158	10.5	3.8	0.5	13.5	1.2	nd	300
Chicken tikka platter, Healthy Options (Walls)	105	2.5	0.7	0.9	7.8	2.5	nd	200
Satay chicken (M&S)	157	4.9	3.1	0.5	18.5	3.9	nd	300
Chicken supreme with rice, MM (Walls)	136	4.1	1.6	0.5	7.2	0.9	nd	200
Tandoori chicken, Healthy Options, (Walls)	127	1.4	0.7	0.6	7.9	1.7	nd	200
Chilli con carne	151	8.5	3	2.3	11	2.8	2.2	250
with rice, Menu Master (Walls)	112	2.2	0.7	1.2	5.6	2	nd	200

All amounts given per 100g, unless otherwise stated

	Calories kcals	Total Fat g	Saturated Fat g	Fibre g	Protein g	Total Sugars g	Iron mg	Sodium (Salt) mg
Coq Au Vin (M&S)	111	4.4	1.1	0.1	15.9	0.4	nd	200
Corned beef hash, potato top (Asda)	78	1.6	0.1	nd	3.9	0.1	nd	600
Cornish pastie	332	20.4	7.4	0.9	8	1.2	1.5	590
Cottage pie, budget (Asda)	97	4.6	1.8	5.7	4.8	2.7	nd	200
Faggots	268	18.5	nd	nd	11.1	Trace	8.3	820
Frankfurters	274	25	nd	0.1	9.5	Trace	1.5	980
(Asda)	296	27	nd	nd	11.8	nd	nd	nd
Gammon steak (M&S)	122	6.2	2.5	0	16.6	nd	nd	1120
Grillsteaks, grilled	305	23.9	11	Trace	22.1	0.5	2.4	650
Haggis, boiled	310	21.7	7.6	nd	10.7	Trace	4.8	770
Hot pot	114	4.5	1.8	1.2	9.4	2.8	1.2	660
Irish stew	123	7.6	3.5	0.9	5.3	1.5	0.6	360
Lamb Tikka Masala (Findus Lean Cuisine)	112	2.5	1.1	1.7	8	2.4	nd	43
Lancashire hotpot (M&S)	77	2.4	1.3	0.5	7.1	1.1	nd	500
Lasagne	102	3.8	1.9	nd	5	2.1	0.7	430
Weight Watchers (Heinz)	93	2.4	1.1	0.5	5.9	2.9	0.6	300
Menu Master (Walls)	132	6.2	2.3	0.6	7.5	3	nd	300
Meatballs in tomato sauce (M&S)	110	4.7	2.5	1.6	10.3	4	nd	500
Liver sausage	310	26.9	7.9	0.5	12.9	0.8	6.4	860

All amounts given per 100g, unless otherwise stated

Savoury Dishes

Savoury Dishes

	Calories	Total Fat	Saturated Fat	Fibre	Protein	Total Sugars	Iron	Sodium (Salt)
	kcals	g	g	g	g	g	mg	mg
Meat paste	173	11.2	nd	0.1	15.2	Trace	2.3	740
Moussaka	184	13.6	4.5	0.9	9.1	2.6	1.1	320
Findus Lean Cuisine	76	2.2	0.6	0.9	5.2	5	nd	300
Paté, liver	319	28.9	8.4	Trace	13.1	0.3	7.1	790
duck with port (Asda)	340	32	11.3	2.6	10.5	2.1	nd	780
Pepperoni (Asda)	489	35	nd	nd	19	nd	nd	nd
Pork pie, individual	376	27	10.2	0.9	9.8	0.5	1.4	720
Ravioli (M&S)	137	6.9	2.5	1	5.8	3.7	nd	400
Salami	491	45.2	nd	0.1	19.3	Trace	1	1850
German peppered (Asda)	341	28.3	12.4	0.3	20.6	1	nd	1400
Sausage roll	477	36.4	13.4	1.2	7.1	1.2	1.2	510
puff pastry (M&S)	384	27.7	9.6	1.3	10	2.5	nd	600
Sausages, beef, fried	269	18	7.2	0.7	12.9	2.4	1.6	1090
beef, grilled	367	32.1	6.7	0.7	13	2.4	1.7	1100
pork, fried	317	24.5	9.4	0.7	13.8	1.7	1.5	1050
pork, grilled	318	24.6	9.5	0.7	13.3	1.8	220	1000
pork (Asda)	226	14.1	5.2	1.1	17.5	1	nd	1100
low fat (Asda)	183	6.8	2.6	1.9	14.9	0.6	nd	1040
liver (Asda)	234	16.4	nd	nd	14.2	nd	nd	nd
Sausages & mash, Menu Master (Walls)	142	7.5	3.5	0.8	4.4	1.6	nd	500

All amounts given per 100g, unless otherwise stated

	Calories (kcals)	Total Fat (g)	Saturated Fat (g)	Fibre (g)	Protein (g)	Total Sugars (g)	Iron (mg)	Sodium (Salt) (mg)
Shepherd's pie	118	6.2	2.4	0.6	8	1	1.2	450
Menu Master (Walls)	92	3.5	1.2	0.8	4.6	0.8	nd	300
Steak in red wine platter, Healthy Options (Walls)	85	2.1	0.4	0.9	6.9	2.5	nd	200
Steak and kidney pie	323	21.2	8.4	0.9	9.1	2.3	2.5	510
Stewed steak, canned in gravy	176	12.5	5.9	Trace	14.8	Trace	2.1	380
Stuffed vine leaves (M&S)	99	3.9	0.5	0.8	2.6	0.2	nd	700
Turkey burgers (Walls)	202	13.1	4.2	0	21	0	nd	400
Wontons (M&S)	368	27.6	10.8	0.8	9.5	1.3	nd	300
SALADS								
Apple (M&S)	50	1.7	0.1	1.5	1.1	7.6	nd	0
Carrot and nut (M&S)	177	13.1	1.9	2	4.3	6	nd	300
Chunky Greek style (Sains)	158	1.7	0.5	nd	2.7	14.2	nd	nd
Coleslaw (M&S)	163	14.8	3.2	0.7	1.1	5.6	nd	1130
Coleslaw lite (M&S)	66	4.7	0.8	1.7	1.3	1.7	nd	300
Coleslaw (Heinz)	130	9.9	1.2	1	1.1	7.1	0.4	400
Crunchy coleslaw (M&S)	45	1.4	0.1	2.5	1.3	6.7	md	0
Egg salad lite (M&S)	74	5	1	1.1	3.6	3.1	nd	100

All amounts given per 100g, unless otherwise stated

Savoury Dishes

Savoury Dishes

FOOD FACTS

	Calories	Total Fat	Saturated Fat	Fibre	Protein	Total Sugars	Iron	Sodium (Salt)
	kcals	g	g	g	g	g	mg	mg
Florida salad (Sains)	206	18.7	1.5	0.9	1.1	7.9	nd	100
Pasta and mushroom (M&S)	196	16	2.6	1.4	3.4	1.1	nd	400
Pasta lite (M&S)	109	6	0.7	0.9	3.1	2	nd	300
Potato (M&S)	193	16.5	3.5	0.5	2.2	1.8	nd	200
Lite potato (M&S)	96	5.6	1.6	1.5	3	1.6	nd	500
Tuna (Sains)	188	17.9	1.7	1	4.5	2	nd	200
Waldorf (Sains)	223	18.1	2.5	2.9	1.5	10.4	nd	400

VEGETABLE DISHES

	Calories	Total Fat	Saturated Fat	Fibre	Protein	Total Sugars	Iron	Sodium (Salt)
Battered onion rings (Asda)	181	8.1	nd	2.2	nd	nd	nd	nd
Cauliflower cheese	105	6.9	3.4	1.3	5.9	3	0.6	200
Weight Watchers (Heinz)	83	2.6	1.4	0.9	5.2	3.8	0.4	200
Chips, see potato in Vegetables								
Crispy crumbed mushrooms (Asda)	261	20.5	nd	nd	4.1	nd	nd	nd
Crispy vegetable fingers (Walls)	164	8.9	4.3	2	3.7	2	nd	400
Cumberland veg pie (M&S)	95	4.1	1.2	0.4	3.8	1.3	nd	800
Golden vegetable nuggets (Walls)	196	8.7	3.7	2	4.5	2.2	nd	600
Layered veg purée (M&S)	59	3.5	2.2	2.3	1.1	1.9	nd	300
Lasagne (M&S)	131	6	2.7	1	7.2	1.7	nd	400

All amounts given per 100g, unless otherwise stated

	Calories (kcals)	Total Fat (g)	Saturated Fat (g)	Fibre (g)	Protein (g)	Total Sugars (g)	Iron (mg)	Sodium (Salt) (mg)
Lentil Dahl (Sains)	96	5.4	3.6	0.3	3.5	1.5	nd	nd
Nut cutlets (Asda)	264	11.9	nd	nd	8.2	nd	nd	nd
Parsnip/Gruyere bake (M&S)	474	32.8	20.9	5.9	13.9	2	nd	800
Potato croquettes (Walls)	158	5.3	2.2	1.2	2.7	1.1	nd	300
Potato nuggets (M&S)	205	11.4	3.4	2.2	3.6	0.5	nd	600
Southern fried (Walls)	202	11.1	4.7	1.1	2.6	0.5	nd	500
Potato waffles (Walls)	191	8.5	3.7	1.9	2.6	0.5	nd	300
Pommes Parisienne (M&S)	73	0.3	0	1.2	1.9	1	nd	0
Ratatouille (M&S)	65	4.8	0.7	1	1.4	3.8	nd	400
Spinach and ricotta canneloni (M&S)	144	9	5.1	1	7	1.6	nd	1110
Spinach ravioli (M&S)	157	5.8	3.8	1.7	8	1.5	nd	400
Vegetable chilli (Asda)	53	0.6	0.2	2.5	2.9	3.1	nd	500
Vegetable Kievs (Walls)	168	8	4.2	1.5	5	2.2	nd	500
Vegetable Medley (M&S)	86	5.5	3.2	2.2	2	2.5	nd	200
Vegetable quarter pounders (Walls)	176	9	4.2	1.8	3.7	1.8	nd	500
Vegetable stir fry (M&S)	29	0.5	0	1.7	2.3	3	nd	0

All amounts given per 100g, unless otherwise stated

Savoury Dishes

Take-away Food

	Calories	Total Fat	Saturated Fat	Fibre	Protein	Total Sugars	Iron	Sodium (Salt)
	Kcals	g	g	g	g	g	mg	mg
BURGER KING								
Whopper	241	13.8	6.3	1	10	4.6	2.3	379
CHINESE								
Beef chow mein	136	6	1.3	nd	6.7	2.4	1.3	590
Crispy Peking duck (Sains)	248	10.7	3.1	0.9	18.2	4.9	nd	461.5
Crispy seaweed (Sains)	688	67.3	4.9	5.1	10.5	18.4	nd	700
Egg fried rice (Asda)	150	4.4	0.5	1.4	4.2	2	nd	700
Spring rolls (M&S)	169	9.1	3.4	2.5	4.2	1.5	nd	600
Sweet and sour chicken (M&S)	117	0.6	0.1	0.7	8.5	9.8	nd	200
INDIAN								
Basmati rice, boiled, (Sains)	130	0.2	0.1	0.8	2.2	0.1	nd	100
Beef curry	137	6.6	3.1	1.2	13.5	4.5	nd	450
with rice	579	4.3	1.9	0.7	8.8	2.6	nd	260

All amounts given per 100g, unless otherwise stated

76

	Calories (Kcals)	Total Fat (g)	Saturated Fat (g)	Fibre (g)	Protein (g)	Total Sugars (g)	Iron (mg)	Sodium (Salt) (mg)
Bombay potatoes (Sains)	80	3	1.6	1.7	2	3.8	nd	294
Chicken curry with rice	149	8.9	4	1.3	12.1	4.4	nd	450
Chicken korma & tumeric rice (Sains)	144	5.5	2.3	0.8	7.8	2.4	nd	250
Chicken korma & pilau rice,	176	8.7	1.8	1	9	2.2	nd	323.5
Weight Watchers	97	2.9	1.3	0.8	6	2.9	0.9	100
Chicken tikka masala (M&S)	197	14	4.7	0.5	13.7	3.4	nd	500
lite tikka (M&S)	139	6.6	2.5	1.4	14.6	5.3	nd	400
Lamb rogan josh (Sains)	185	13.2	1.8	1.4	12.2	4.4	nd	294
Onion bhaji (Asda)	281	14.8	1.5	1.5	6.1	5.9	nd	300
Pilau rice (Sains)	129	1	0.4	0.8	2.2	0.1	nd	100
Samosas	593	56.1	7.8	1.2	5.1	1	0.8	33
Veg curry (M&S)	87	6.3	2.1	1.5	2.1	3.3	nd	300
Vegetable samosas, fried	472	41.8	5.2	1.8	3.1	1.9	0.8	200
not fried (Asda)	136	"1,1"	0.2	2.6	3.9	3	nd	600
Vegetable tikka masala (Sains)	95	6.2	2.9	0.8	3.2	4.8	nd	400
Jacket potato & cheddar cheese (Sains)	137.6	5.9	3.5	1.4	4.72	0.3	nd	320
Jacket potato & chicken tikka (Sains)	110	3.7	2	1.9	4.5	2.2	nd	200
Lamb kofta kebabs grilled (Sains)	197	12.2	4.8	1.5	15.9	1.8	nd	800

All amounts given per 100g, unless otherwise stated

Take-away Food

Take-away Food

FOOD FACTS

	Calories	Total Fat	Saturated Fat	Fibre	Protein	Total Sugars	Iron	Sodium (Salt)
	Kcals	g	g	g	g	g	mg	mg
KENTUCKY FRIED CHICKEN								
original recipe chicken	208	nd	nd	nd	17.5	nd	nd	nd
Colonel's classic burger with lettuce & mayo	247	11.9	nd	nd	12.8	nd	nd	nd
Colonel's fillet burger	227	9.4	nd	nd	15.4	nd	nd	nd
Fries	227	9.8	nd	nd	4.1	nd	nd	nd
Corn on the cob	94	2.1	nd	nd	2.9	nd	nd	nd
Barbecue beans	83	0.8	nd	nd	5	nd	nd	nd
McDONALDS								
Apple pie	270	17	5.5	5.6	5.3	12.2	nd	260
Banana milkshake	118	2.2	1.6	nd	2.8	17.7	nd	94
Big Mac	239	13.1	6.3	1.9	12.9	3.5	nd	450
Fillet-o-Fish	233	10.5	4.5	2.3	10.7	3.1	nd	450
French fries	345	21.5	4.7	8.7	4.8	1.2	nd	150
Hamburger	244	8.6	4	2.7	13.9	5.7	nd	450
McChicken sandwich	231	9.9	1.8	1.3	11.4	4.9	nd	500
Quarter pounder with cheese	254	13.6	6.4	2.5	14.6	5.3	nd	450

All amounts given per 100g, unless otherwise stated

	Calories	Total Fat	Saturated Fat	Fibre	Protein	Total Sugars	Iron	Sodium (Salt)
	Kcals	g	g	g	g	g	mg	mg
Chicken McNuggets	254	13.6	5.1	0.9	17.7	0.6	nd	500
Pizza – Deluxe	338	16.6	6.2	1.7	15.3	3.7	nd	700
PIZZAS								
Cheese & tomato (Sains)	224	8	4.7	1.2	11.9	1.3	nd	400
Chicago ham & mushroom (Sains)	216	5.7	2.8	1.2	11.3	3.8	nd	546
Garlic mushroom, thin & crispy (Sains)	286	12.2	6.4	2.5	12.4	1.5	nd	600
Spicy sausage, deep & crispy (Sains)	293	14.7	6	1.5	12.5	2.1	nd	790
Tuna & prawn Provencal, thin & crispy (Sains)	233	8.1	5.4	1	13.9	3.9	nd	605
SANDWICHES								
bacon, tomato and lettuce (Asda)	205	8.4	nd	3.1	7.9	nd	nd	nd
avocado and prawn (M&S)	241	16.1	3.5	2.1	8.1	3.8	nd	500
cheese coleslaw (M&S)	262	15.8	7.3	2.3	11.1	5.6	nd	400
cheese & celery (M&S)	287	19.7	7.8	1.9	10.1	2.5	nd	500
soft cheese & celery (M&S)	136	5.4	3.6	2.5	7.3	2.7	nd	300
cheese and tomato (Asda)	212	8.8	nd	2.3	10	nd	nd	nd

All amounts given per 100g, unless otherwise stated

Take-away Food

Take-away Food

Food	Calories	Total Fat	Saturated Fat	Fibre	Protein	Total Sugars	Iron	Sodium (Salt)
	Kcals	g	g	g	g	g	mg	mg
cheese ploughman's (M&S)	249	16.3	7.8	2.3	8.8	4	nd	600
chicken & lemon low cal (M&S)	157	5.2	2	2.6	12.4	1.7	nd	400
chicken & salad roll (M&S)	263	16.4	5.1	1	11.9	2.2	nd	500
chicken tikka (Asda)	228	11.3	nd	1.9	10.8	nd	nd	nd
tikka filled pitta (M&S)	175	7.2	2.3	1.3	9.9	1	nd	300
egg and bacon (M&S)	245	15	4.2	2.1	13.9	1.1	nd	900
egg mayonaise and cress (Asda)	209	10.6	nd	3.8	10.3	nd	nd	nd
egg and cress (M&S)	189	9.1	3.9	2	9.4	1.9	nd	600
med rare roast beef (M&S)	209	10.6	4.5	3	15.5	4.4	nd	700
prawn and mayonnaise (Asda)	167	5.9	nd	6.9	9.4	nd	nd	nd
prawn, ham & chick low cal (M&S)	149	5.2	1.6	2.2	10.1	2.2	nd	500
prawn & ham BLT (M&S)	277	17.8	5.1	2	10.7	2.6	nd	700
tuna and coleslaw, low cal (Asda)	175	6.3	1.2	1.7	9.7	nd	nd	470
roast chicken & yoghurt, low cal (Asda)	197	6.6	2.4	2.8	12.6	nd	nd	320
smoked salmon (M&S)	213	8.2	4.1	2.2	15.4	1.5	nd	700
tuna (M&S)	216	12.2	3	3.9	12.6	1	nd	500

All amounts given per 100g, unless otherwise stated

Soups

All amounts given per 100g, unless otherwise stated

	Calories	Total Fat	Fibre	Calcium	Iron	Sodium (Salt)	Beta-carotene	Vitamin C
	Kcals	g	g	mg	mg	mg	mcg	mg
Asparagus soup, canned	36	1.7	0.3	11.9	0.3	402	108	1.1
cream of (Heinz)	70	3.5	0.3	17.6	0.3	722	108	1.1
cream of (Heinz)	51	3.7	0.2	nd	nd	400	nd	nd
Beef broth	53	1.2	nd	23.5	0.8	739	nd	0
Beef soup (Heinz)	40	1.8	0.2	nd	0.3	500	55	0
Broccoli soup, cream of	14	0	0	0	0	722	0	0
Celery soup, Weight Watchers (Heinz)	22	0.7	0.2	nd	0.1	300	214	0
Celery soup, cream of	70	4.4	0.8	17.6	0	722	75	0
Chicken soup, canned	88	6.2	0.3	17.6	0	722	75	0
cream of, canned	16	0.6	0	3.7	0.2	318	nd	1.8
noodle, dried with water	58	3.8	0.2	27	0.4	460	0	0
vegetable	20	0.3	0.2	3	0.2	370	0	0
& mushroom (Heinz)	38	2.2	0.1	nd	0.7	400	nd	0
Clam chowder	63	2.2	0.6	7.4	0.4	401	312	1.8
Consommé (Cross & Blackwell)	20	Trace	Trace	nd	nd	300	nd	nd
Farmhouse veg (Heinz)	45	0.4	0.9	nd	0.7	500	528	0
French onion soup	32	0.9	0.8	11	0.7	237	108	1.6
Heinz	26	0.2	0.4	nd	0.1	400	3	0

Soups and Sauces

Soups and Sauces

	Calories	Total Fat	Fibre	Calcium	Iron	Sodium (Salt)	Beta-carotene	Vitamin C
	Kcals	g	g	mg	mg	mg	mcg	mg
Gazpacho	53	1.8	0.4	17.6	0.3	792	0	2.1
Green pea soup	23	0.9	nd	9.8	0.4	485	nd	1.3
Leek and potato soup (M&S)	239	20.5	1.6	nd	nd	700	nd	nd
Lentil soup	141	2.6	1.1	0	1.3	722	48	0
canned (Asda)	99	3.8	1.1	38	1.2	45	325	1
Minestrone soup, dried with water	44	0.4	0.6	500	nd	nd	nd	nd
minestrone soup (M&S)	43	1.4	1.1	nd	nd	400	nd	0
Mushroom, cream of, canned	23	0.7	nd	9	0.2	430	nd	0
(M&S)	66	4.7	0.7	nd	nd	300	nd	nd
Weight Watchers (Heinz)	24	0.6	0.1	ns	0.1	300	9	0
Oxtail soup, canned	53	3.8	nd	30	0.3	470	0	0
dried with water	44	1.7	nd	40	1	440	0	0
Potato & leek (Heinz)	34	0.6	0.5	nd	0.2	400	415	1
Sausage and bean soup (M&S)	58	1.3	1.2	nd	nd	600	nd	nd
Seven veg soup (Heinz)	34	0.4	0.8	nd	0.3	400	832	3
Scotch Broth (Heinz)	44	0.8	0.9	nd	0.4	400	745	0
Tomato soup, canned	23	0.7	nd	9	0.2	430	0	0
cream of, canned	68	1.5	1	11	1.4	695	336	2
cream of (M&S)	82	5.6	0.6	nd	nd	300	nd	nd
cream of (Heinz)	57	2.8	0.7	nd	0.4	400	459	0

All amounts given per 100g, unless otherwise stated

	Calories	Total Fat	Fibre	Calcium	Iron	Sodium (Salt)	Beta-carotene	Vitamin C
	Kcals	g	g	mg	mg	mg	mcg	mg
tomato and herb (M&S)	72	4	0.4	nd	nd	0.34	nd	nd
tomato, Weight Watchers, (Heinz)	25	0.7	0.1	nd	0.3	400	366	4
dried with water	55	3.3	nd	17	0.4	460	210	Trace
Vegetable soup, canned (Asda)	31	0.5	nd	14	0.2	390	N	Trace
Vichyssoise	37	0.7	1.5	17	0.6	500	18	Trace
	38	0.5	0.8	nd	nd	500	nd	nd
Winter veg (Heinz)	43	0	0.9	nd	0.8	500	680	0
SAUCES								
Apple sauce (Heinz)	61	0.2	1.5	nd	0.2	0	13	2
Barbecue sauce, American, (Heinz)	94	0.1	0.5	nd	0.6	1120	506	3
Bearnaise sauce	75	1.8	N	19	0.9	810	520	7
Branston sandwich pickle (Cross & Blackwell)	122	0.1	1.7	nd	nd	1150	nd	nd
Brown sauce (Asda)	79	0	nd	nd	nd	200	nd	nd
Carbonara sauce (M&S)	213	19.6	2.3	nd	3.1	980	nd	nd
Cheese sauce, with whole milk	99	0	0.7	43	0.2	450	40	Trace
with semi-skimmed milk	197	14.6	0.2	240	0.2	450	105	1
cheese sauce (M&S)	150	11.6	0.1	nd	nd	300	nd	nd

All amounts given per 100g, unless otherwise stated

Soups and Sauces

Soups and Sauces

Food	Calories (Kcals)	Total Fat (g)	Fibre (g)	Calcium (mg)	Iron (mg)	Sodium (Salt) (mg)	Beta-carotene (mcg)	Vitamin C (mg)
Curry paste, medium, (Sains)	181	12.6	10.3	nd	nd	2400	nd	nd
French dressing lite (M&S)	179	12.6	0.2	240	0.2	450	93	1
Hot chilli sauce (Heinz)	383	40	0.4	nd	nd	800	nd	nd
Guacamole (M&S)	102	0.1	1.2	nd	nd	1160	nd	nd
Gravy, brown from granules	149	14.3	0.3	nd	nd	2110	nd	nd
virtually fat free (100ml) instant	649	72.1	0	12	0.3	930	2	0
gravy mix (Sains)	32	Trace	Trace	nd	nd	500	nd	nd
Hollandaise sauce	29	0.7	nd	25.6	0.1	417	nd	0
Horseradish (Sains)	98	2.8	3.2	nd	nd	900	nd	nd
Houmous (M&S)	275	19.9	3.2	nd	nd	600	nd	nd
Lite Italian dressing (M&S)	522	57.6	0.1	nd	nd	300	nd	nd
Italian vinaigrette, low fat, (Heinz)	31	0	0.1	nd	0.3	300	17	0
Mango chutney	153	8.4	2.5	43	0.5	910	Trace	Trace
Marmite	285	10.9	0.9	23	2.3	1090	130	1
Mayonnaise, thick & creamy, (Sains)	738	80	0	nd	nd	400	nd	nd
low calorie	386	39	nd	nd	nd	nd	nd	nd
Mint sauce	691	75.6	0	8	0.3	450	100	Trace
Mustard, brown	87	Trace	nd	120	7.4	700	Trace	Trace
Dijon	75	4.4	2.7	84.2	2	1252	0	0

All amounts given per 100g, unless otherwise stated

	Calories	Total Fat	Fibre	Calcium	Iron	Sodium (Salt)	Beta-carotene	Vitamin C
	Kcals	g	g	mg	mg	mg	mcg	mg
Mustard, English (M&S)	226	15.9	1	nd	nd	3500	nd	nd
yellow	96	6.7	0.9	131	1.9	1381	0	1
wholegrain (M&S)	179	13	2	nd	nd	8	nd	nd
Peanut butter (M&S)	620	50.9	6.5	nd	nd	400	nd	nd
Pesto (Sains)	385	39.7	2	nd	0	900	0	0
Piccalilli	126	6.3	0.8	20	0	2516	22	5
Ploughman's Piccalilli (Heinz)	89	0.3	0.5	nd	0.5	700	54	0
Pickle	123	0	1.5	0	0	581	nd	nd
mixed pickle (M&S)	28	0.1	1.7	nd	nd	800	nd	nd
sweet pickle (M&S)	129	0	0.9	nd	nd	500	0	nd
Red wine & mushroom sauce (Sains)	51	1	0.3	nd	0.7	300	nd	0
Salad cream (Heinz)	325	26.5	0	18	0.5	1110	17	0
Salsa, green	15	nd	1.1	12.1	0.3	1040	1005	18.1
Satay sauce	348	31	nd	nd	nd	760	nd	nd
Seafood sauce	456	45	nd	26	nd	127	84	0.4
Soy sauce	151	1.3	4.9	19	1.7	5720	0	0
Sweet and sour sauce	64	nd	nd	nd	2.7	352	0	16.2
Tabasco	159	0	0.1	5.6	0.4	900	nd	nd
Taramasalata (M&S)	506	50	0.6	nd	nd	nd	nd	nd

All amounts given per 100g, unless otherwise stated

Soups and Sauces

Soups and Sauces

	Calories	Total Fat	Fibre	Calcium	Iron	Sodium (Salt)	Beta-carotene	Vitamin C
	Kcals	g	g	mg	mg	mg	mcg	mg
Tartar sauce	272	21.7	nd	5	1	440	61	68
Thousand Island dressing (Heinz)	284	22.6	0.4	nd	nd	1130	nd	nd
low fat (Heinz)	79	4.3	0.1	nd	0.3	600	64	2
Tomato ketchup	98	trace	0.9	25	1.2	1120	230	2
Heinz	101	0.1	0.8	nd	nd	1120	nd	nd
low sugar, low salt	78	0.2	nd	nd	nd	nd	nd	nd
Tomato pasta sauce	98	Trace	0.9	25	1.2	1120	230	2
Tzatziki (M&S)	122	7	0.4	nd	nd	300	nd	nd
White sauce, with whole milk	47	1.5	N	23	0.7	410	nd	Trace
with semi-skimmed milk	150	10.3	0.2	130	0.2	400	77	Trace
White wine sauce (M&S)	119	11.4	0.5	nd	nd	300	nd	nd
Worcester sauce (Holbrooks)	92	0.2	nd	nd	nd	1140	nd	nd
Yogurt & herb dressing (Heinz)	76	4.3	0	nd	0.2	300	24	0

All amounts given per 100g, unless otherwise stated

SAVOURY SNACKS

	Calories	Total Fat	Saturated Fat	Fibre	Total Sugars	Iron	Sodium (Salt)	Vitamin C
	Kcals	g	g	g	g	mg	mg	mg
Banana chips	518	33.5	28.9	6.6	nd	1.2	7	6.3
Bombay mix	503	32.9	4	6.2	2.3	3.8	770	Trace
Asda	530	37.5	nd	5.5	nd	nd	nd	nd
Cashew nuts, roasted and salted	611	50.9	10.1	3.2	13.2	6.2	290	0
Cheese straws (M&S)	580	43.3	18.4	1.3	2	nd	1120	nd
mini cheese biscuits (M&S)	534	30.4	17.5	2	5.6	nd	900	nd
Corn Snacks	519	31.9	11.8	1	4.6	0.8	1130	Trace
Fruit and nut assorted (M&S)	525	38.6	6.7	1.7	26.4	nd	50	nd
luxury assorted nuts (M&S)	647	60.1	6.5	5.2	6.5	nd	400	nd
Grissini sticks (M&S)	449	19.2	7.9	2.7	3.9	nd	700	nd
Olives, green in brine	103	11	1.7	2.9	Trace	1	2250	0
Peanuts, salted	602	53	9.5	6	3.8	1.3	400	0
dry roasted	589	530	8.9	6.4	3.8	2.1	790	0
Peanuts and raisins	435	26	4.6	4.4	34	2.1	27	Trace
Pistachio nuts, salted	606	52.8	6.7	10.8	nd	3.2	780	7.3
Popcorn, plain	387	5	0.6	8	nd	2.7	3	0
caramel coated	432	12.8	3.6	6	nd	1.7	205	0
butter flavour	370	22.2	3.7	7.4	nd	1.3	630	0

All amounts given per 100g, unless otherwise stated

Savoury Snacks

Savoury Snacks

	Calories	Total Fat	Saturated Fat	Fibre	Total Sugars	Iron	Sodium (Salt)	Vitamin C
	Kcals	g	g	g	g	mg	mg	mg
Potato crisps, plain	538	35.4	4.2	3.8	nd	1.7	1070	27
barbeque flavour	489	32.4	8	3.2	nd	1.9	750	33.8
Brannigans, roast beef & mustard, (KP)	507	30.3	12.1	7.7	0.9	nd	700	nd
cheese flavour	493	27.1	8.6	4.8	nd	1.8	792	53.9
cheese and onion reduced fat (M&S)	470	23.1	10.6	5.7	2.4	nd	1100	nd
crinkles (M&S)	530	36.7	13.4	7.4	0.3	nd	700	nd
hoops	523	32	N	2.6	0.5	1	1070	3
Kettle chips	556	38.4	9.4	4.8	nd	1.5	655	8.1
gourmet chips, barbecue, (Sains)	500	29.4	4.1	5.1	0.9	nd	600	nd
low fat	472	20.8	4.2	4.8	nd	1.3	489	25.7
lower fat salt & vinegar (KP)	470	22.8	9.1	4.3	1	nd	1110	nd
reduced fat potato rings (M&S)	429	15.4	7.1	10.5	6.9	nd	1120	nd
McCoys original crisps (KP)	528	34	13.6	5.4	0.8	nd	500	nd
potato rings (M&S)	538	33	13.2	2.5	0.6	nd	1110	nd
potato triangles (Asda)	484	24.2	nd	17.5	nd	nd	nd	nd
ready salted (M&S)	551	36.8	14.7	4	0.7	nd	500	nd
salt & vinegar (M&S)	518	35.6	13	7	3.1	nd	1150	nd
Skips, prawn cocktail, (KP)	512	28.4	13	1.4	7.2	nd	1130	nd
Pretzels	389	4.5	0.9	2	nd	1.5	1680	0
Ricecakes	376	3	13.1	1.7	nd	1.8	116	1.7

All amounts given per 100g, unless otherwise stated

	Calories	Total Fat	Saturated Fat	Fibre	Total Sugars	Iron	Sodium (Salt)	Vitamin C
	Kcals	g	g	g	g	mg	mg	mg
Sesame sticks (M&S)	492	27.9	8.6	2.7	2	nd	700	nd
Shelled nuts (M&S)	522	50.3	8.6	8.7	5.4	nd	0	nd
Sunshine mix (Asda)	nd	31.7	nd	8	nd	nd	nd	nd
Tortilla chips	459	22.6	4	4.9	1.2	1.6	850	Trace
light (M&S)	494	25	4.6	4	1.6	nd	300	nd
sour cream and onion (M&S)	505	28.1	4.9	3.7	2.5	nd	400	nd
Tropical selection (Asda)	410	18	nd	6	nd	nd	nd	nd
Twiglets	383	11.7	4.9	10.3	1.1	2.9	1330	Trace
Waffles (M&S)	473	22.7	1.1	0	39.2	nd	2500	nd

All amounts given per 100g, unless otherwise stated

89

Savoury Snacks

Biscuits, Cakes and Puddings

FOOD FACTS

BISCUITS

	Calories	Total Fat	Saturated Fat	Fibre	Total Sugars	Calcium	Iron	Vitamin C
	Kcals	g	g	g	g	mg	mg	mg
Coconut crinkle (Sains)	497	26.9	16.6	5.1	26	nd	nd	nd
Cream crackers	440	16.3	2.2	Trace	110	1.7	0.7	22
Double choc cookies (M&S)	513	27.5	14.7	2.3	28.8	nd	nd	nd
Crispbread, rye	321	2.1	11.7	3.2	45	3.5	3	35
light (M&S)	360	5	1.9	5.2	2.5	nd	nd	nd
Crisp rolls (M&S)	385	8	1.7	9	0.8	nd	nd	nd
Custard creams	61	2.9	1.8	0.2	3.7	nd	nd	nd
Digestive biscuits, plain	471	20.9	2.2	13.6	92	3.2	0.5	13
M&S	510	23.8	10.6	2.6	20.8	nd	nd	nd
high fibre (M&S)	489	22.9	10.1	6.2	15.1	nd	nd	nd
chocolate	493	24.1	2.2	28.5	84	2.1	1	11
Flapjacks	484	26.6	2.7	35.5	37	2.1	1.5	100
Garibaldi	389	9.4	4.1	nd	4.1	nd	nd	nd
Gingernut biscuits	456	15.2	1.4	35.8	130	4	0.5	4
ginger snaps (M&S)	443	12.8	4.9	1.5	40	nd	nd	nd
Jaffa cakes	363	10.5	nd	57.2	55	1.5	0.3	5
M&S	378	8.2	4.3	0.8	59.1	nd	nd	nd
Lemon puff creams (M&S)	549	35.9	10	2.9	14.8	nd	nd	nd

All amounts given per 100g, unless otherwise stated

	Calories	Total Fat	Saturated Fat	Fibre	Total Sugars	Calcium	Iron	Vitamin C
	Kcals	g	g	g	g	mg	mg	mg
Malted milk	498	22	10.5	2.2	nd	nd	nd	nd
Marzipan (Asda)	435	13.3	1.1	1.7	68.8	nd	nd	nd
Nice biscuits (Tesco)	470	18.6	10.3	3	25.1	nd	nd	nd
Oatcakes	441	18.3	nd	3.1	54	4.5	2.3	26
Duchy originals oaten biscuits	456	20.1	2.7	7.7	10.6	nd	nd	nd
Raisin & pecan cookies (M&S)	502	28.2	10.2	2.4	25.8	nd	nd	nd
Rich tea biscuits (Tesco)	455	15.7	7.1	2.4	23.6	nd	nd	nd
cream (M&S)	493	21.4	11.5	1.5	31.9	nd	nd	nd
Scottish oat cakes (M&S)	413	12.6	5.4	8.5	2.7	nd	nd	nd
fingers (M&S)	466	14.5	6.4	2.3	21.3	nd	nd	nd
Shortbread	498	26.1	1.9	17.1	91	1.3	0.4	7
Slender plan bars, apple & raisin (Nestlé)	350	12.2	7.5	8.8	11.4	nd	nd	nd
chocolate flavour (Nestlé)	452	20.6	7.4	3.9	nd	nd	nd	nd
date & peanut (Nestlé)	425	21.3	11.6	9.8	9.4	nd	nd	nd
6 Stollen slices (M&S)	405	17.7	8.1	1.3	39.2	nd	nd	nd
Milk choc wafer fingers (M&S)	548	29.6	9.7	0.8	38.4	nd	nd	nd
thick choc wafer bars (M&S)	504	30.8	15	1	46.5	nd	nd	nd
m/choc caramel (M&S)	486	23.5	10.4	0.5	48.7	nd	nd	nd
Wheaten crackers (M&S)	460	22	16	5	4.5	nd	nd	nd

All amounts given per 100g, unless otherwise stated

Biscuits, Cakes and Puddings

Biscuits, Cakes and Puddings

CAKES

	Calories	Total Fat	Saturated Fat	Fibre	Total Sugars	Calcium	Iron	Vitamin C
	Kcals	g	g	g	g	mg	mg	mg
Angel layer cut cake (Tesco)	337	11.5	6.6	0.8	38.4	nd	nd	nd
Apple pies (M&S)	337	13.1	7.7	1.6	27	nd	nd	nd
Apple tart (M&S)	233	10.2	4.7	1.6	22.5	nd	nd	nd
Bakewell tarts (M&S)	438	21.8	8.1	1.3	36.6	nd	nd	nd
Baklava (M&S)	389	18.6	8.1	1.9	28.8	nd	nd	0
Banana cake	435	9.2	2.3	1	nd	45.8	0.8	0
Battenburg cake	370	17.5	4.7	nd	34	87	1.1	nd
M&S	350	10	1.8	1.4	55.8	nd	nd	nd
Birthday cake (M&S)	368	13.8	6.5	0.5	54.4	nd	nd	nd
Blackforest gateau, frozen (M&S)	268	14	8.1	0.8	25	nd	nd	nd
Cappucino log, frozen (M&S)	227	12.1	7.5	0	23.9	0	0.9	2.8
Carrot cake	352	21.3	3.9	1.1	nd	nd	nd	nd
Carrot orange slice (M&S)	421	25.7	7	1.2	36.2	nd	nd	Trace
Cheesecake	297	9.6	5.9	1.2	33.1	120	1.6	9
blackcurrant, Weight Watchers (Heinz)	152	4.2	2.2	0.6	14.9	nd	0.6	nd
choc chip (M&S)	391	23.6	14.2	0.2	35.4	nd	nd	nd
strawberry (walls)	233	11.3	nd	nd	nd	111	nd	nd
Chocolate Krispies	464	18.6	10.7	0.3	40.7	28	4	0

All amounts given per 100g, unless otherwise stated

	Calories	Total Fat	Saturated Fat	Fibre	Total Sugars	Calcium	Iron	Vitamin C
	Kcals	g	g	g	g	mg	mg	mg
Chocolate fudge cake	391	21.7	6.2	1.9	nd	0	1.6	0
M&S	439	25.9	11.3	1.7	41.6	nd	nd	nd
Birthday cake (M&S)	433	27	13.1	0	32.9	nd	nd	nd
choc layer gateau, frozen (M&S)	327	18.2	16.5	0.6	25	nd	nd	nd
white choc torte (M&S)	378	24.3	18.3	0.2	31.6	nd	nd	nd
creme caramel (M&S)	197	10.8	5.9	0.1	20.3	nd	nd	nd
Cream slices (M&S)	387	22.9	9.3	0.6	29.3	nd	nd	nd
Chelsea buns (M&S)	305	9	2.9	2.1	24	nd	nd	nd
Choux buns (M&S)	317	22.2	9.7	0.3	15.4	nd	nd	nd
Croissants, all butter (M&S)	350	20	12.6	1.4	5.4	nd	1.1	0
Crumpets, toasted	199	1	0.1	2	1.9	120	nd	nd
M&S	186	1	0.2	1.4	1.7	nd	1.9	0
Currant buns	296	7.5	nd	nd	15.1	110	0.8	0
Custard tarts, individual	277	14.5	5.6	1.2	12.8	95	nd	0
egg custard tarts (M&S)	232	11.5	3.8	0.5	16.9	nd	1.3	nd
Danish pastries	374	17.6	5.6	1.6	28.5	92	1.2	0
Doughnuts, ring	397	21.7	6.3	nd	15.3	76	1.2	0
jam	336	14.5	4.3	nd	18.8	72	nd	nd
USA style (M&S)	316	10.2	0.7	1.8	15.3	nd	1.2	nd
Eccles cakes	475	26.4	10.1	1.6	41.1	79		0

All amounts given per 100g, unless otherwise stated

Biscuits, Cakes and Puddings

Biscuits, Cakes and Puddings

	Calories	Total Fat	Saturated Fat	Fibre	Total Sugars	Calcium	Iron	Vitamin C
	Kcals	g	g	g	g	mg	mg	mg
Eccles cakes, M&S	401	17.8	11.3	1	39.3	nd	nd	nd
Eclairs	396	30.6	16.1	0.8	6.6	87	1.1	Trace
milk choc eclairs (M&S)	418	32.7	16.5	0.5	20.2	nd	nd	nd
Fondant Fancies (Asda)	337	10.1	nd	nd	nd	nd	nd	0
Fancy iced cakes, individual	407	14.9	9.3	nd	54	44	1.4	0
Fruit cake	354	12.9	5.8	nd	43.1	60	1.7	nd
Asda, all butter, iced	348	8	nd	3.6	nd	nd	nd	nd
M&S, rich	362	10.5	3.9	3.1	61.6	nd	nd	nd
Ginger cake (M&S)	326	10.1	1.9	0.9	30.9	nd	nd	nd
Hot cross buns (Allinson)	260	6.8	2.4	4.6	21.6	nd	nd	nd
Iced finger buns (M&S)	319	8.8	7.3	0.9	23.1	nd	nd	nd
Jam tarts (Tesco)	385	14.6	3.9	4.6	40.5	nd	nd	nd
Lemon slices (M&S)	381	16.2	3.4	0.7	46.5	nd	nd	nd
Lemon torte, frozen (M&S)	274	16	10	0.4	18	nd	nd	nd
Madeira cake	368	13	4.8	nd	36	72	1.7	Trace
Meringues (M&S)	389	0	0	0	90.8	nd	nd	nd
Meringue nests	373	nd	nd	nd	nd	nd	nd	nd
Mince pies	393	16.9	8.8	0.9	36.5	42	1.1	0
Asda	423	20.4	7.4	2.1	28.1	75	1.5	0

All amounts given per 100g, unless otherwise stated

	Calories	Total Fat	Saturated Fat	Fibre	Total Sugars	Calcium	Iron	Vitamin C
	Kcals	g	g	g	g	mg	mg	mg
Mince Pies M&S	378	15	4.1	1	40.4	nd	nd	nd
Mississippi mud pie (M&S)	233	15.1	7.1	0.5	14.8	nd	nd	nd
Muffins, raisin and bran (M&S)	235	1.9	0.4	3.2	10.9	nd	nd	nd
Orange and carrot cake (M&S)	323	14	9.5	1.4	27.4	nd	nd	nd
Fresh cream palmiers (M&S)	525	43.8	32.9	0.9	11.8	nd	nd	nd
Parkin (M&S)	345	10.6	2.3	1.7	36.2	nd	nd	nd
Pastry, flaky, cooked	355	14.1	nd	1.8	nd	nd	nd	Trace
shortcrust, cooked	560	40.6	14.7	1.8	0.9	84	1.3	0
wholemeal, cooked	521	32.3	11.7	2.2	1.1	99	1.5	nd
Pavlova, strawberry, (Sains)	261	8	5.3	1	2.4	nd	nd	nd
Pikelets (M&S)	186	0.9	0.2	0.4	1.4	nd	nd	nd
Profiteroles (M&S)	405	35.6	19.8	0.4	14	nd	nd	0
Rock cake	499	32.9	11.8	6.3	1.5	28	2.8	nd
Scones, plain	240	7.9	nd	0.6	nd	nd	nd	nd
fruit	362	14.6	4.9	1.9	5.9	180	1.3	Trace
potato (M&S)	178	4.5	1.4	4.1	0.8	nd	nd	nd
wholemeal	316	9.8	3.3	nd	16.9	150	1.5	Trace
Scotch pancakes (M&S)	303	11.5	1.5	1.5	18.2	nd	nd	nd
Sponge cake	326	14.4	4.8	5.2	5.9	110	2.3	Trace

All amounts given per 100g, unless otherwise stated

Biscuits, Cakes and Puddings

Biscuits, Cakes and Puddings

	Calories	Total Fat	Saturated Fat	Fibre	Total Sugars	Calcium	Iron	Vitamin C
	Kcals	g	g	g	g	mg	mg	mg
Sponge cake								
with butter icing	459	26.3	8	0.9	30.4	66	1.2	0
fatless	490	30.6	9.4	0.6	37.1	47	0.9	0
chocolate gateau (M&S)	381	16.7	10.3	0.5	43.8	nd	nd	nd
chocolate roll (M&S)	379	15	8.2	0.8	40.5	nd	nd	nd
raspberry gateau (M&S)	374	16.3	10.3	2	41.9	nd	nd	nd
toffee (M&S)	347	9.7	4.6	0.4	53.6	nd	nd	nd
Victoria sandwich (M&S)	396	21.4	12.4	0.7	29.3	nd	nd	nd
Swiss rolls, chocolate, individual	294	6.1	1.7	0.9	30.9	75	1.7	0
Asda	337	11.3	nd	nd	41.8	77	1.1	0
jam swiss roll (M&S)	254	2.4	0.8	1.6	44.7	nd	nd	nd
Tarte Tatin (M&S)	357	25.1	9.6	1.2	18.1	nd	nd	nd
strawberry & cream cake, frozen (M&S)	322	21.7	13.4	0.1	21.3	nd	nd	nd
Teacakes, toasted	371	15	nd	0.9	nd	nd	nd	nd
Tin roof (Walls)	320	20.8	nd	nd	nd	137.6	nd	nd
Tiramisu	329	8.3	nd	nd	16.4	98	2.9	Trace
M&S	250	20.3	13.6	0.5	13	nd	nd	nd
tiramisu gateau (M&S)	324	21.8	10.3	0.3	21.3	nd	nd	nd
Toffee cake	382	21.2	12.4	0.6	30.3	nd	nd	nd
Treacle tart (M&S)	408	14.8	5	1.5	41.4	nd	nd	nd

All amounts given per 100g, unless otherwise stated

	Calories	Total Fat	Saturated Fat	Fibre	Total Sugars	Calcium	Iron	Vitamin C
	Kcals	g	g	g	g	mg	mg	mg
Trifle sponges	314	1.8	nd	nd	nd	nd	nd	nd
Viennese fancies	510	28.9	17.3	1.4	33.2	nd	nd	nd
Walnut slab (M&S)	417	22.8	9.9	1.1	34.9	nd	nd	nd
Bread & butter pudding (Tesco)	181	5.4	3.6	0.5	19.7	nd	nd	nd
Caramel dessert (M&S)	125	4.1	3	0	20	nd	nd	nd
Christmas pudding	242	10.6	5.6	0.9	22.2	68	160	0
Crème brulée	329	11.8	6.1	1.7	46.2	340	1.2	Trace
Creme caramel (Chambourcy)	110	1.5	0.5	0	20.3	nd	nd	nd
Crumble, fruit	109	2.2	nd	nd	18	94	Trace	0
fruit, wholemeal	198	6.9	2.1	1.7	21.3	49	0.6	3
Custard, with whole milk	193	7.1	2.1	2.7	21.4	32	0.9	3
with skimmed milk	117	4.5	2.8	Trace	11.4	130	0.1	1
canned	79	0.1	0.1	Trace	11.6	140	0.1	1
virtually sugar free instant custard mix (Asda)	402	8.3	7.8	nd	18.5	nd	nd	nd
Delight, banana flavour (Asda)	458	15.5	15	0.1	62.4	nd	nd	nd
virtually sugar free chocolate flavour (Asda)	418	15.8	14.7	0.5	15	nd	nd	nd
sugar free, banana flavour (Asda)	444	17.3	16.6	0.1	15.7	nd	nd	nd
Fool, gooseberry (M&S)	141	7.9	4.8	1	14.6	nd	nd	nd

All amounts given per 100g, unless otherwise stated

Biscuits, Cakes and Puddings

Biscuits, Cakes and Puddings

FOOD FACTS

All amounts given per 100g, unless otherwise stated

	Calories	Total Fat	Saturated Fat	Fibre	Total Sugars	Calcium	Iron	Vitamin C
	Kcals	g	g	g	g	mg	mg	mg
Fruit pie, pastry top	95	3	1.7	0.1	12.3	100	0.2	0
pastry top and bottom	186	7.9	2.9	1.7	15.6	48	0.5	5
apple	260	13.3	4.8	1.8	12	59	0.8	3
blackcurrant (Tesco)	389	13.4	3.3	3.1	23.9	nd	nd	nd
wholemeal	262	13.3	4.8	2.6	12.5	70	1.2	72
Fruit salad, canned	251	13.6	4.9	3.5	12.2	29	1.3	4
Gateau, black forest (Asda)	337	16.8	9.5	0.4	32.3	60	0.9	0
Ice cream, vanilla	317	20.8	nd	nd	nd	nd	nd	nd
chocolate	194	9.8	6.4	Trace	22.1	130	69	1
choc red calorie (Heinz)	132	5.1	3.4	0.4	15.4	nd	0.5	0
choc soft (M&S)	97	4.3	2	0	11.7	nd	nd	nd
choc truffle (M&S)	160	7.3	3.7	0.3	19.1	nd	nd	nd
hazelnut (M&S)	196	13.7	7.4	0	14	nd	nd	nd
neapolitan soft (M&S)	92	4	3.2	0	11.1	nd	nd	nd
neapolitan red calorie (Heinz)	133	5.7	3.8	0.3	14.4	nd	0.3	1
luxury vanilla (M&S)	178	12	7.4	0	14.5	nd	nd	nd
non-dairy, vanilla	186	10.2	nd	nd	nd	nd	nd	nd
Arctic roll	178	8.7	4.4	Trace	19.2	120	76	1
choc ice	200	6.6	3.1	Trace	25.3	90	0.7	0
choc ice, dark (Asda)	277	17.5	10.8	Trace	nd	130	0.1	nd

	Calories	Total Fat	Saturated Fat	Fibre	Total Sugars	Calcium	Iron	Vitamin C
	Kcals	g	g	g	g	mg	mg	mg
Ice cream, choc ice, light	340	25.4	nd	nd	nd	nd	nd	nd
sorbet, lemon	260	12.9	6.7	nd	25.5	120	nd	nd

INDIVIDUAL ICE CREAMS AND LOLLIES

	Calories	Total Fat	Saturated Fat	Fibre	Total Sugars	Calcium	Iron	Vitamin C
Choc bar, Cadbury, Dairy Milk, (Walls)	358	21.5	nd	nd	nd	154.8	nd	nd
choc bar, dark and golden, (Walls)	315	20	nd	nd	nd	121.8	nd	nd
Magnum almond (Walls)	343	22.8	nd	nd	nd	151.8	nd	nd
Magnum, dark chocolate, (Walls)	318	21.2	nd	nd	nd	115.54	nd	nd
Magnum, white chocolate, (Walls)	318	21.2	nd	nd	nd	144.16	nd	nd
Cornetto, choc & nut, (Walls)	301	16.8	nd	nd	nd	135.8	nd	nd
strawberry (Walls)	240	9.6	nd	nd	nd	104.4	nd	nd
Feast (Walls)	377	28.6	nd	nd	nd	130	nd	nd
Mini Juice, apple, (Walls)	84	Trace	nd	nd	nd	2.8	nd	nd
orange (Walls)	84	Trace	nd	nd	nd	4.2	nd	nd
banana, (Walls)	133	1	nd	nd	nd	159.6	nd	nd
Orange Fruitie (Walls)	83	Trace	nd	nd	nd	4.4	nd	nd
Sparkles, orange (Walls)	54	Trace	nd	nd	nd	1.8	nd	nd
Tub, dairy vanilla (Walls)	184	8.8	nd	nd	nd	153.6	nd	nd

All amounts given per 100g, unless otherwise stated

Biscuits, Cakes and Puddings

Biscuits, Cakes and Puddings

	Calories	Total Fat	Saturated Fat	Fibre	Total Sugars	Calcium	Iron	Vitamin C
	Kcals	g	g	g	g	mg	mg	mg
Tub, dream flake (Walls)	248	12.8	nd	nd	nd	179.2	nd	nd
family Cream of Cornish, vanilla, (Walls)	190	9	nd	nd	nd	160	nd	nd
Gino Ginelli choc & nut slice (Walls)	209	11.4	nd	nd	nd	150.1	nd	nd
Gino Ginelli, toffee fudge (Walls)	98.8	10.5	nd	nd	nd	144.4	nd	nd
Gino Ginelli, Tutti Frutti (Walls)	198	8.1	nd	nd	nd	133.2	nd	nd
Gino Ginelli, honeycomb choc (Walls)	225	10.8	nd	nd	nd	153	nd	nd
golden vanilla, sliceable (Walls)	183.6	9.18	nd	nd	nd	142.8	nd	nd
Soft scoop, rum & raisin (Walls)	190	7.6	nd	nd	nd	131.1	nd	nd
Too good to be true, dbl choc, (Walls)	152	0.8	nd	nd	nd	163.2	nd	nd
vanilla/strawberry ripple (walls)	144	0.8	nd	nd	nd	139.2	nd	nd
Triple Brownie Overload (Haagen Dazs) 1 bar	400	31	nd	nd	nd	nd	nd	Trace
Viennetta (Walls)	243	14.4	nd	nd	nd	142.2	nd	nd
white chocolate (Walls)	288	18	nd	nd	nd	136.8	nd	Trace
Jelly	131	Trace	Trace	0	34.2	2	18	Trace
raspberry (Rowntree)	81	Trace	0	0.8	20.2	nd	nd	nd
strawberry (Rowntree)	67	Trace	0	0.5	16.7	nd	nd	nd
Lemon meringue pie	61	0	0	0	15.1	7	5	0

All amounts given per 100g, unless otherwise stated

	Calories	Total Fat	Saturated Fat	Fibre	Total Sugars	Calcium	Iron	Vitamin C
	Kcals	g	g	g	g	mg	mg	mg
Meringue	319	14.4	5	0.7	24.8	45	0.9	3
with cream	379	Trace	Trace	0	95.4	4	0.1	0
Milk pudding, with whole milk	376	23.6	14.7	0	40	39	Trace	Trace
with skimmed milk	129	4.3	2.7	0.1	10.7	130	0.1	1
Mousse, chocolate	93	0.2	0.1	0.1	10.9	130	0.1	1
chocolate (Asda)	139	5.4	nd	nd	17.5	97	1.6	0
chocolate orange Aero (Chambourcy)	211	8.6	4.8	0.1	25.6	180	nd	nd
fruit	197	7.7	nd	nd	4.7	nd	nd	nd
Pancakes	137	5.7	nd	nd	18	120	Trace	Trace
Rice pudding, canned	301	16.2	7.1	0.8	16.2	110	0.8	1
Sponge pudding	89	2.5	1.6	0.2	8.2	93	0.2	0
Spotted dick (M&S)	303	13.9	4.8	2.5	25.2	nd	nd	nd
spotted dick with custard (M&S)	229	6.9	2.8	1.5	26.5	nd	nd	nd
Sticky toffee pudding (M&S)	283	10.6	4.1	0.9	39.9	nd	nd	nd
Raspberry torte (Heinz)	132	4.7	4	0.5	14.6	nd	0.3	1
Treacle tart	340	16.3	5.1	1.1	18.9	84	1.1	Trace
Trifle	368	14.1	5.1	1.1	33.6	62	1.4	0
fresh cream strawberry (Asda)	166	9.2	5.2	0.5	15	68	0.3	4
sherry (M&S)	181	11	7	0.3	17.1	nd	nd	nd
Triple choc delights (M&S)	131	6	4	0.1	15.7	nd	nd	nd

All amounts given per 100g, unless otherwise stated

Biscuits, Cakes and Puddings

Sugars, Jams and Confectionery

SUGARS, JAMS AND CONFECTIONERY

	Calories	Total Fat	Saturated Fat	Fibre	Total Sugars	Calcium	Iron	Vitamin C
	Kcals	g	g	g	g	mg	mg	mg
Chocolate, milk, average	529	30.3	17.8	56.5	220	1.6	120	0
plain, average	525	29.2	16.9	59.5	38	2.4	11	0
white, average	529	30.9	18.2	58.3	270	0.2	110	0
Chocolate brazils	575	44.7	nd	nd	nd	nd	nd	nd
After dinner mints (M&S)	440	20.5	12.9	63.3	nd	nd	20	nd
Buttons, milk choc, (M&S)	537	33.5	21.3	53.6	nd	nd	100	nd
Bounty	473	26.1	21.2	53.7	110	1.3	180	0
Chunky choc cappuccino bar (M&S)	524	33.3	20.3	43.7	nd	nd	0	nd
Chunky milk choc bar (M&S)	529	30.4	19	55.3	nd	nd	120	nd
Champagne truffle bar (M&S)	497	28	17.6	50	nd	nd	0	nd
Coins, milk choc (M&S)	504	33	18.1	52	nd	nd	80	nd
Cointreau liqueur bar (M&S)	479	26.1	14	53.4	nd	nd	60	nd
Creme eggs	385	16.8	nd	58	120	0.8	55	0
Crunchie	490	24.2	nd	nd	nd	nd	nd	nd
Chunky hazelnut choc bar (M&S)	563	37.3	16.2	44.2	nd	nd	100	nd
Dairy Milk (Cadbury)	520	28.7	nd	nd	nd	nd	nd	nd
Dark choc bar (Green & Blacks)	586	39	nd	nd	40	nd	nd	nd
Flake	530	30.7	nd	nd	nd	nd	nd	nd

All amounts given per 100g, unless otherwise stated

	Calories	Total Fat	Saturated Fat	Total Sugars	Calcium	Iron	Sodium (Salt)	Vitamin C
	Kcals	g	g	g	g	mg	mg	mg
Kit Kat	499	26.6	13.8	46.8	200	1.5	110	0
Mars Bar	441	18.9	10	65.8	160	1.1	150	0
Maya Gold bar (Green & Blacks)	586	39	nd	nd	40	nd	nd	nd
Milk choc bar (Green & Blacks)	541	31	nd	nd	40	nd	nd	nd
Milky Way	397	15.8	8.3	62.6	120	1.7	100	0
Mini eggs (M&S)	571	37.7	27.5	48.6	nd	nd	60	nd
Plain mountain bar (M&S)	514	34	20	48	nd	nd	100	nd
Smarties	456	17.5	10.3	70.8	150	1.5	58	0
Swiss truffles (M&S)	514	35.6	20.4	43.1	nd	nd	60	nd
Twix	480	24.5	12	47.7	110	1.1	190	0
Walnut whip (M&S)	481	26.8	12.9	55.5	nd	nd	120	nd
Wispa	540	33.2	nd	nd	nd	nd	nd	nd
Chocolate spread (Sains)	324	1.6	1	72.1	nd	nd	100	0
Ginger preserve	269	0	0	55.7	nd	nd	300	0
Golden syrup	298	0	0	79	26	1.5	270	0
Glucose syrup	318	0	0	40.2	8	0.5	150	0
Hazelnut & chocolate spread	517	31	10.4	53.3	8	nd	0	nd
Honey	288	0	0	76.4	nd	0.4	11	nd
Canadian (M&S)	300	0	0	80	5	nd	110	0
comb honey	281	4.6	0	74.4	8	0.2	7	0

All amounts given per 100g, unless otherwise stated

Sugars, Jams and Confectionery

Sugars, Jams and Confectionery

FOOD FACTS

	Calories	Total Fat	Saturated Fat	Fibre	Total Sugars	Calcium	Iron	Vitamin C
	Kcals	g	g	g	g	mg	mg	mg
Jam, apricot (M&S)	266	0.1	0	64.9	nd	nd	490	nd
pure fruit (Asda)	270	0	0	59.4	nd	nd	500	nd
simply blackcurrant (M&S)	114	0	0	23.2	nd	nd	0	nd
simply strawberry (M&S)	97	0	0	21.3	nd	nd	0	nd
strawberry (Sains)	268	0.2	Trace	65	nd	nd	<100	nd
strawberry, reduced sugar (Sains)	135	0.1	Trace	32.3	nd	nd	<100	nd
Lemon curd	283	5.1	nd	40.4	9	0.5	65	Trace
Marmalade	261	0	0	69.5	35	0.6	18	10
medium cut (M&S)	247	0	0	63.9	nd	nd	40	nd
Sugar, white	394	0	0	99.9	2	Trace	Trace	0
demerara	394	0	0	99.9	53	0.9	6	0
Sweets, boiled	327	Trace	0	86.9	5	0.4	25	0
butter mintoes (M&S)	391	6.8	4.1	83.4	nd	nd	500	nd
chocolate peanuts (M&S)	543	34.2	14.3	43.7	nd	nd	70	nd
chocolate raisins (M&S)	405	13.2	8.5	65.6	nd	nd	80	nd
coconut ice (M&S)	396	10.1	8.4	61.8	nd	nd	0	nd
Dolly mixtures (M&S)	377	1.5	1.4	89.8	nd	nd	80	nd
fruit gums (M&S)	320	0	0	68.1	nd	nd	0	nd
fruit gums	172	0	0	42.6	360	4.2	64	0
fruit pastilles (Sains)	334	Trace	0	75.1	nd	nd	Trace	nd

All amounts given per 100g, unless otherwise stated

	Calories	Total Fat	Saturated Fat	Total Sugars	Calcium	Iron	Sodium (Salt)	Vitamin C
	Kcals	g	g	g	g	mg	mg	mg
Sweets,								
Jelly Babies, mini (M&S)	330	0	0	78.5	nd	nd	0	nd
Liquorice Allsorts	313	2.2	0.6	67.2	63	8.1	75	0
Sweets,								
Liquorice Allsorts (M&S)	350	4.7	4.1	66.1	nd	nd	190	nd
marzipan	404	14.4	1.2	67.6	66	0.9	20	0
milk choc caramels (M&S)	495	22.6	16.3	39.5	nd	nd	300	nd
mint humbugs (M&S)	410	5.2	4	70.6	nd	nd	160	nd
strong mints (M&S)	391	0	0	97.5	nd	nd	0	nd
peanut brittle (M&S)	500	29.4	6.8	32	nd	nd	140	nd
pastilles	253	0	0	61.9	40	1.4	77	0
peppermints	392	0.7	N	99.1	7	0.2	9	0
popcorn, all butter, (M&S)	415	12.8	7.8	67.6	nd	nd	400	nd
toffees, mixed	430	17.2	13.7	70.1	95	1.5	320	0
traditional toffees (M&S)	513	29.7	21.6	59.4	nd	nd	290	nd
Turkish delight	295	0	0	68.6	10	0.2	31	0
Turkish delight choc bar (M&S)	353	8.5	5.5	50.9	nd	nd	0	nd
Treacle, black	257	0	0	67.2	500	9.2	96	0

All amounts given per 100g, unless otherwise stated

Sugars, Jams and Confectionery

Drinks and Juices

DRINKS AND JUICES

	Calories Kcals	Total Fat g	Total Sugars g	Caffeine mg	Beta-carotene mcg	Vitamin C mg	Folic Acid mcg
Bitter lemon (Sains)	36	Trace	8.7	0	nd	nd	nd
Cocoa with whole milk	76	4.2	6.6	2.9	20	Trace	5
with semi-skimmed milk	57	1.9	6.8	2.9	9	1	5
Coffee, freshly brewed, black	2	Trace	0.3	58.8	0	0	Trace
instant, black	100	0	6.5	32	0	0	Trace
coffee substitute	5	0	0	0	0	0	Trace
Nescafé granules (Nestlé)	94	Trace	11	4000	nd	nd	nd
Nescafé Blend 37, granules (Nestlé)	85	Trace	11	4500	nd	nd	nd
Nescafé Decaf, granules (Nestlé)	107	Trace	13.5	100	nd	nd	nd
Cordial, lite orange, (M&S)	75	0	4.7	0	nd	nd	nd
Chocolate mint (M&S)	345	16	21.1	nd	nd	nd	nd
Elderflower water (M&S)	6	0	1.4	0	nd	nd	nd
Fizzy drinks, cola, average	40	0	10.6	20	0	0	0
cola, diet (nutrasweet)	1	0	0	14	0	0	0
Coca Cola	43	0	10.6	nd	nd	nd	nd
Cherry Coca Cola	45	0	11.2	nd	nd	nd	nd
Caffeine-free, diet Coca Cola	0.4	0	0.03	nd	nd	nd	nd
Diet Coca Cola	0.4	0	0.03	nd	nd	nd	nd

All amounts given per 100g, unless otherwise stated

	Calories	Total Fat	Total Sugars	Caffeine	Beta-carotene	Vitamin C	Folic Acid
trad cola (M&S)	40	0	10.7	nd	nd	nd	nd
cream soda	51	0	nd	0	0	0	0
cream soda, sugar free peach & rasp (Sains)	0.3	Trace	Trace	0	nd	nd	nd
Fanta Orange	47	0	8.9	0	nd	nd	nd
Five Alive Citrus	50	0	12	0	nd	nd	nd
dry ginger ale (Sains)	24	Trace	5.7	0	nd	nd	nd
ginger beer	34	0	8.7	0	0	0	0
lemonade	40	0	10.2	0	0	0	0
trad lemonade (M&S)	199	0	11.8	0	nd	nd	nd
Lilt	45	0	11	0	nd	nd	nd
Diet Lilt	4	0	0.6	0	nd	nd	nd
Lucozade	67	0	8.6	nd	0	3	Trace
Mango Lilt	45	0	11.1	0	nd	nd	nd
orangeade	48	0	nd	0	0	0	0
pear spring water (M&S)	6	0	1.4	0	0	nd	nd
root beer	41	0	11.9	0	4	0	0
Sprite	43	0	10.5	0	nd	nd	nd
tonic water	34	0	nd	0	0	0	0
diet Indian tonic water (Sains)	0.2	Trace	Trace	0	nd	nd	nd
	Kcals	g	g	mg	mcg	mg	mcg

All amounts given per 100g, unless otherwise stated

Drinks and Juices

Drinks and Juices

	Calories	Total Fat	Total Sugars	Caffeine	Beta-carotene	Vitamin C	Folic Acid
	Kcals	g	g	mg	mcg	mg	mcg
Horlicks, with whole milk	99	3.9	10	nd	18	Trace	nd
with semi-skimmed milk	81	1.9	10.2	nd	8	1	nd
Hot chocolate powder, with whole milk	90	4.1	10.3	2.9	nd	Trace	5
with semi-skimmed milk	71	1.9	10.5	2.9	nd	1	5
Juices, apple	47	0.1	10.9	0	Trace	14	4
apple (M&S)	220	0	12.2	0	nd	nd	nd
apple supreme (M&S)	220	0	12.2	0	nd	nd	nd
apple & mango (M&S)	235	0	13	0	nd	nd	nd
supreme apple & mango (M&S)	235	0	13	nd	nd	nd	nd
apricot nectar	56	0.1	nd	0	nd	1	1
carrot	40	0.2	nd	0	15413	9	4
grape	46	0.1	11.7	0	Trace	Trace	1
grapefruit	33	0.1	8.3	0	1	31	6
pink grapefruit (M&S)	178	0	10.7	0	nd	nd	nd
jaffa orange (M&S)	155	0	9.3	0	nd	nd	nd
lemon	7	Trace	1.6	0	12	36	13
orange	36	0.1	8.8	0	17	39	20
orange 'C', Libby (Nestlé) 100ml	37	Trace	9.1	0	nd	40	nd
pineapple	41	0.1	10.5	0	8	11	8
prune	71	Trace	13.4	0	nd	4.1	Trace

All amounts given per 100g, unless otherwise stated

	Calories	Total Fat	Total Sugars	Caffeine	Beta-carotene	Vitamin C	Folic Acid
	Kcals	g	g	mg	mcg	mg	mcg
Juices,							
strawberry coolcrush (M&S)	70	0.3	14.5	0	nd	nd	nd
tomato	14	Trace	3	0	200	8	10
V8 vegetable juice	21	0	3.3	0	700	20	21
Malted milk drink	97	7.8	nd	nd	0	1.8	6.2
Milk, flavoured	68	1.5	9.4	0	8	Trace	2
Nesquik, chocolate (Nestlé) 100ml	90	3.5	11.2	nd	nd	nd	nd
Nesquik, strawberry (Nestlé) 100ml	69	1.7	10	nd	nd	nd	nd
Ovaltine, with whole milk	97	3.8	nd	0	18	Trace	nd
with semi-skimmed milk	79	1.8	nd	0	8	1	5
Tea, brewed	1	Trace	0	20	nd	0	nd
fresh Darjeeling	0	0	0	30	nd	nd	1
herbal, brewed	1	0	0	13	nd	0	Trace
instant	1	0	0	0	0	0	0
Water	0	0	0	0	0	nd	nd
Yoghurt drink, pina colada, (M&S)	110	0.1	55.5				

All amounts given per 100g, unless otherwise stated

109

Drinks and Juices

Alcoholic Drinks

	Calories	Total Sugars	Alcohol
	Kcals	g	g
Beer, draught bitter	32	2.3	3.1
mild draught	25	1.6	2.6
Brandy, Cognac	243	0	35
Cider, dry	36	2.6	3.8
sweet	42	4.3	3.7
Cocktail, Bloody Mary	77	nd	9.4
daiquiri	186	nd	23.2
gin and tonic	71	nd	6.3
martini	198	nd	26.5
mint jelup	71	nd	9.7
pina colada	186	nd	23.2
rum sour	165	0	21.5
scotch and soda	84	0	11.2
screwdriver	82	nd	6.6
tequila sunrise	109	nd	10.9
Fortified wine, dessert	153	nd	15.3
Madeira	105	nd	15
port	157	12	15.9
sherry, dry	140	6.1	15
vermouth, dry	105	5.4	15

All amounts given per 100g, unless otherwise stated

110

	Calories	Total Sugars	Alcohol
vermouth, sweet	167	39.7	18
Lager, average	31	1.8	nd
bottled	28	1.5	3.2
Liqueur, anisette	370	nd	35
apricot brandy	320	30	30
Benedictine	345	nd	33
curacao	270	28.4	30
creme de menthe	372	nd	29.8
kahlua	336	39.1	21.7
Spirits, gin / rum / vodka / whisky			
100 proof	295	0	42.5
90 proof	263	0	37.9
80 proof	230	0	33.4
Wine, all varieties	71	1.5	9.3
champagne	70	nd	9.2
red	68	0.3	9.5
rosé	71	1.5	9.3
white	68	0.6	9.3

All amounts given per 100g, unless otherwise stated

Alcoholic Drinks

HOW TO ORDER YOUR BOXTREE BOOKS BY LIZ EARLE

LIZ EARLE'S QUICK GUIDES

Available Now

☐	1 85283 542 7	Aromatherapy	£3.99
☐	1 85283 544 3	Baby and Toddler Foods	£3.99
☐	1 85283 543 5	Food Facts	£3.99
☐	1 85283 546 X	Vegetarian Cookery	£3.99

Available from September 1994

☐	0 7522 1619 8	Evening Primrose Oil	£3.99
☐	0 7522 1614 7	Herbs for Health	£3.99
☐	1 85283 984 8	Successful Slimming	£3.99
☐	1 85283 989 9	Vitamins and Minerals	£3.99

ACE PLAN TITLES

☐	1 85283 518 4	Liz Earle's Ace Plan The New Guide to Super Vitamins A, C and E	£4.99
☐	1 85283 554 0	Liz Earle's Ace Plan Weight-Loss for Life	£4.99

All these books are available at your local bookshop or can be ordered direct from the publisher. Just tick the titles you want and fill in the form below.

Prices and availability subject to change without notice.

Boxtree Cash Sales, P O Box 11, Falmouth, Cornwall TR10 9EN

Please send cheque or postal order for the value of the book, and add the following for postage and packing:

UK including BFPO – £1.00 for one book, plus 50p for the second book, and 30p for each additional book ordered up to a £3.00 maximum.

OVERSEAS including Eire – £2.00 for the first book, plus £1.00 for the second book, and 50p for each additional book ordered.

OR please debit this amount from my Access/Visa Card (delete as appropriate).

Card Number

AMOUNT £ ....

EXPIRY DATE ....

SIGNED ....

NAME ....

ADDRESS ....

....